# THE DRUKNEN COOBOOK

*Milton Crawford*

SQUARE PEG

Published by Square Peg 2013

2 4 6 8 10 9 7 5 3 1

First published in Great Britain in 2013 by Square Peg
Random House, 20 Vauxhall Bridge Road,
London SW1V 2SA

www.vintage-books.co.uk

Addresses for companies within The Random House Group Limited can be
found at: www.randomhouse.co.uk/offices.htm

The Random House Group Limited Reg. No. 954009

A CIP catalogue record for this book is available from the British Library

ISBN 9780224098472

The Random House Group Limited supports the Forest Stewardship Council®
(FSC®), the leading international forest-certification organisation. Our books
carrying the FSC label are printed on FSC®-certified paper. FSC is the only
forest-certification scheme supported by the leading environmental organisations,
including Greenpeace. Our paper procurement policy can be found at
www.randomhouse.co.uk/environment

Typeset in Adobe Caslon Pro
Printed and bound in China by C&C Offset Printing Co., Ltd.

If you're struggling to read this, then you probably shouldn't be trying to cook.

Cooking tends to involve plenty of hazards such as sharp knives, hot surfaces, boiling water and the very real possibility of fire. The author and publisher would like to point out that it is you – rather than us – who is responsible for any kind of inebriated state that you might find yourself in. We are therefore unable to accept any responsibility either for your drunken condition, or for any accidents or misadventures you may have while using this cookbook. That said, we urge you to take every possible precaution to ensure you do not harm yourself or others in any way. We have pointed out dangers, and included safety instructions in the recipes where applicable, but suggest that you also use your own common sense. And, if you think that you may, at least temporarily, be lacking in that commodity, then we politely suggest that you get out of the kitchen and let someone else do the cooking for you. Or get a takeaway. Or go to bed.

Alcohol diminishes our inhibitions. It makes us more likely to be adventurous; to speak to someone we wouldn't normally speak to, do something we normally wouldn't do, go somewhere we normally wouldn't go. It tempts us to redefine the limits we unconsciously ring-fence our lives with: to abandon caution, to speak honestly rather than gloss over the truth, to extend metaphors beyond the pale. In other words alcohol offers, however dishonestly, a taste of freedom, which is one of the reasons why it can be so dangerously addictive. It also offers the opportunity for other forms of experimentation and adventure in different areas of our lives – and, for the purposes of this book, I'll mainly be talking about the kitchen.

Whether it be on returning home from the pub after a quick drink with colleagues on a weekday, or having invited friends round at 3 a.m. after a hard night on the tiles, the tipsy gastronome has the opportunity to explore tastes and flavours that they might previously have dismissed, but that now suddenly make more sense.

Intensity is important – the dipsomaniacal gourmet embraces strong, bold flavours: salty, smoky, spicy, unctuous and garlicky. We are interested in umami and pickles, the sharp slice of raw onion cutting through cheese, the powerful punch of chilli spiking pork fat. It may be a little crude, but then the inspiration for these recipes comes from bar snacks, street food and takeaways rather than Michelin-starred restaurants – food that is prepared quickly to deliver a big and satisfying hit.

Practicality also has to play a role: the recipes contained within this book are designed to be simple enough for a person who is moderately incapacitated, and quick enough to prepare before the eyes glaze over. Safety is also a consideration – deep-fried food has not been included, for example.

But this is not just a cookbook for complete inebriates, whose compass is not aligned with their mentis (whatever the hell that is). They are already well catered for by kebab shops, curry houses and chip shops. This is more a playful tome for all kinds of gastronomic adventure; alcohol is the schooner for our voyage on the seas of culinary creativity, booze is our boat across oceans of bacchanalian kitchen-craft…

Now, what was I saying about extending metaphors…?

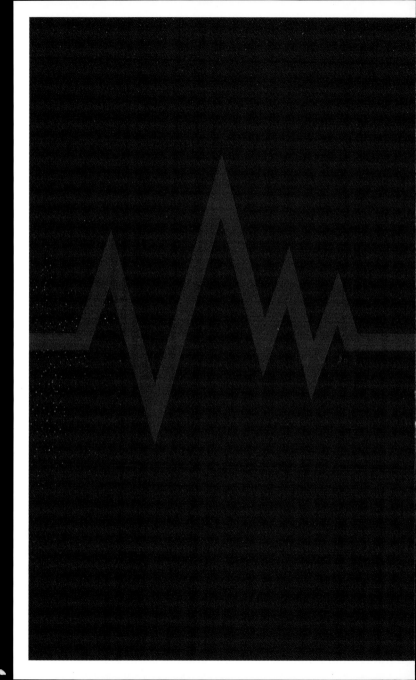

# WHAT'S THE DRUNKEN DIAGNOSIS?

—

Are you three
sheets to the
wind, or have
the sheets blown
away entirely?

Hint: if you've no idea what I'm talking about,
drop the book right now and walk away.

Use this handy diagnostic section to work out if you're a bubble or a newt, a puppy or a penguin. This will help you determine which recipes you may be able to tackle. It will be easier and more accurate (and more fun) if a companion is on hand to adjudicate, as your own judgement may be less than objective. The tests all assume that some level of drinking has taken place. Complete sobriety does not register on the scale so, teetotallers, please close the book and consider instead giving it to that uncle who always seems rather too eager to pour a G&T at four in the afternoon.

# THE ONE-LEGGED STANDING TEST

—

Instead of simply administering a breath test, some sadistic American cops like to humiliate potential drink-drivers by making them do all kinds of ridiculous gymnastics at the side of the road while other drivers cruise by, laughing at the circus unfolding on the sidewalk. You may choose your own audience while you do this test. Regardless of the results, please do not consider driving afterwards.

Stand with your hands by your sides and raise one foot (either will do) approximately 15 centimetres above the ground in front of you. While holding this position, look at the ceiling and count to 30.

How long did you last?

(a) the full distance
(b) the mid-twenties
(c) how long would you like me to last?
    Okay, yes, I admit, the -teens
(d) under 10
(e) how do you balance? Wobble, wobble
(f) aahhhh! Thud

# THE REFLEX RULER TEST

As you get more and more drunk, your reflexes get poorer and poorer. Even with relatively low blood-alcohol levels from just a couple of drinks, your reflexes are half as good as they were when you were sober. There is an easy way to check the quality of your reflexes that you may remember from school: the reflex ruler test. You will need a standard 30-centimetre ruler and someone to administer this test.

Your partner will need to hold the ruler vertically at approximately shoulder height. Hold out your hand approximately 10 centimetres below the bottom of the ruler. (Depending on the punctiliousness of your partner, they may decide to measure this precisely.) Position your finger and thumb so that you are ready to grasp the ruler should it fall (it will, shortly.)

Your partner should ask: 'Are you ready?'

Once you have replied in the affirmative, he or she may drop the ruler. Your task is to catch it as quickly as possible between your finger and thumb. Technically you should do this a few times to rule out freak results and take the average.

How many centimetres did the ruler drop before you caught it?

(a) less than 10cm
(b) 10–15cm
(c) as Einstein said: 'Not everything that counts can be counted, and not everything that can be counted counts'. If I have to put a figure on it: 15–20cm?
(d) 20–30cm
(e) I used that ruler to measure the distance between my eyes
(f) what ruler?

# THE
# MEMORY
# TEST

—

Neural function declines in all kinds of ways due to the presence of alcohol in the bloodstream. One obvious symptom is memory recall. What was the name of that film? Who was that person you both knew at school? Who passed out on the pavement after that party?

Test how much your memory has deteriorated by playing a game of Granny goes to market. You'll need someone to play it with. You know this game? All you have to do is to say 'Granny goes to market and she bought…' Then you begin listing the items that Granny picked up, taking it in turns with your companion(s), one at a time. It could be anything, so it might go: an aubergine, a ball of wool, a cagoule, a dog, an Ecstasy pill, a fennel bulb, a gigolo, a hammer, an iguana… The items do not have to be in alphabetical order. I just did that because I thought it was funny (as I write this I've drunk three pints of Guinness and an espresso martini). The person who can remember the most items, wins.

How many items could you remember?

(a) 10–15
(b) 8–10
(c) as Mark Twain said: 'If you tell the truth, you don't have to remember anything.' Okay, somewhere between 5 and 8
(d) less than 5, I think
(e) who the hell is Granny?
(f) bleurrgh

# THE MOOD TEST

—

One symptom of drunkenness is what is called the 'labile mood', sometimes called 'emotional dysregulation', or, to you and I, mood swings. You might recognise this from that person who is perfectly nice when they're sober, but can suddenly become a monster when they're drunk.

This primitive little test attempts to assess how balanced (or unbalanced) your mood is right now. Someone insults you. It's not a terrible insult. It's along the lines of: 'You bloody idiot'. Or: 'You know what, you really are a bit of a loser'. Or: 'I'm really not sure about that cardigan'. Something like that.

What's your reaction?

(a) come on, life's too short to be nasty to one another
(b) I love being me; if you got to know me, I'm sure you'd love me too
(c) Sir (or Madam), may I say: you seem to be speaking an infinite amount of nothing
(d) forget about it: give us a hug and let's party!
(e) get me another drink!
(f) come here: I'm going to f___ you up.

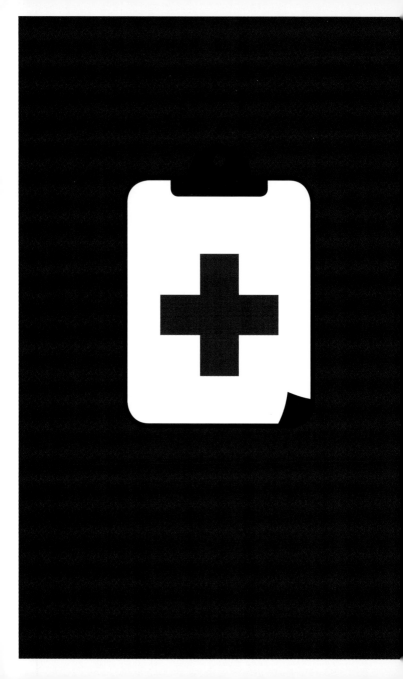

# THE RESULTS

—

If you've made it this far, then well done…

...it already suggests that you're not too horrendously smashed to manage basic tasks in the kitchen. But read on to find out the official diagnosis and how capable I feel you may be of tackling some proper cooking. When sharp knives and hot water are involved, it's probably best not to over-extend yourself, so please hedge on the side of caution, rather than adventure.

# The
# Bubble

If you answered mainly (a) then you are probably experiencing 'The Bubble'.

You have barely moved beyond sobriety but have imbibed just enough to have all the lightness and fizz of a bubble rising inexorably upwards in a flute of champagne. You are tinged with rose-tinted euphoria, warmed by the joy of humanity, buoyed by the oxygen of life. The glass is half full.

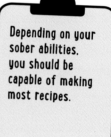

Depending on your sober abilities. you should be capable of making most recipes.

# The
# Puppy

If you answered mainly (b) then it's quite likely that right now you're 'The Puppy'.

Puppies are generally so full of confidence that everyone they meet instantly falls in love with them. You are in this puppy-like state at the moment, thinking that you are irresistibly charismatic/charming/beautiful/handsome (choose any or all of the above). In fact, your coordination and reflexes are already suffering, even though your senses feel extraordinarily heightened.

You should be able to make most recipes and, indeed, may feel as though it's all a bit too easy. But watch out — over-confidence can also be a significant handicap to success.

# The
# Oscar

If you answered mainly (c) then you're quite clearly in a state I describe as 'The Oscar'.

'Champagne for my real friends, real pain for my sham friends.' Oscar Wilde was full of such witty asides and by now you feel as though Wilde would struggle to keep up with your own brand of sparkling conversation. You're so sharp right now that people might cut themselves on you. Or, at least, that's what you think, as you are also beginning to slur a little and not everyone might be as impressed with your wit as you so evidently are.

If you are ready to take time-out from talking, then you could attempt some of the easy to medium difficulty recipes – but you may have a problem concentrating on some of the more difficult ones.

# The
# Duracell

If you answered mainly (d) then the evidence suggests you're 'The Duracell'.

A primal energy has been unleashed within you and now you are an unstoppable force of nature that is prepared to party for as long as it takes to… well, who knows what – there is neither rhyme nor reason to your incorrigibility. The difficulty is that this energy lacks coordination and sudden enthusiasms are forgotten as quickly as they came to you in the first place. Hang on, come back! This is for you. Right, now don't start making something to eat then give up halfway through.

Stick to the easiest
of the recipes.
and think about
getting someone to
help you.

# The
# Penguin

If you answered mainly (e) then it seems that you may be 'The Penguin'.

As you become afflicted with a bunch of terms that can be found near the beginning of any reputable medical dictionary (ataxia, apraxia, agraphia), you may acquire that same kind of unsteadiness witnessed in the flightless birds of the southern hemisphere as they waddle through snow drifts and ice, occasionally falling flat on their sleek bellies. Whereas real penguins are able to slide effortlessly along on their tummies, though, you will most likely find yourself stranded, and, quite probably, in some pain.

It may be that toast is the best thing you can turn your hand to right now. any more that that and toast may be what you'll become.

# The
# Newt

If you answered mainly (f) then I reckon you're 'The Newt'.

Detailed investigation usually reveals compelling reasons for the origins of seemingly obscure phrases, but 'pissed as a newt' remains somewhat enigmatic. Something is clear: the newt means you have plumbed the depths. You will not be able to read these sentences. They are lost on you. I have literally wasted minutes writing words that will be incomprehensible to my readers. Now I know how Will Self and Salman Rushdie must feel.

If you are capable of reading this. then please follow this instruction:

STAY OUT OF
THE KITCHEN.

# The
# Tipsy Store
# Cupboard

It's good to have a range of 'super-ingredients' on hand so that you can quickly inject serious flavour into your food when you most need it.

Here are some suggestions for some store-cupboard staples:

Indian spices
(cumin, coriander
— ground and
whole — turmeric,
cayenne pepper,
cinnamon bark,
cloves and curry
leaves)

Pickles — pickled
eggs, gherkins,
cornichons,
capers, jalapeños

Smoked paprika

Harissa paste

Anchovies

Garlic

Dried garlic

Powdered onion

Root ginger

Lemon grass

Lime leaves

Fresh and
dried herbs

Saffron

Soy sauce

Cox's Original
Bloody Mary
Spicer

Worcestershire
Sauce

Wahaca Smoky
Chipotle Chilli
Sauce

Fish sauce

Various fresh
chillies

Chipotle chillies

Liquid hickory
smoke

Cheese

Wine and sherry
(for cooking
and, if you feel
like it, drinking,
too)

# The recipes

## THE DRUNKEN CARNIVORE
—

Chargrilled smoky harissa chicken 36

Cheat's cassoulet 38

Chicken livers, bacon and mushrooms on toast 40

The Philly cheesesteak sandwich 42

Seared rare beef fillet with Parmesan 44

Spicy Thai-style pork burgers with a cucumber and peanut salad 46

## STEAMING HOT
—

Calcutta-style seekh kebab rolls 52

Chicken tikka kebabs with kebab-shop salad 54

Henry and Lisa's Montserrat-style chicken wings 56

Pakistani lamb kofta 58

Chargrilled vegetable and cheese quesadilla 60

Quick couscous chicken biryani 62

## WELL-OILED
—

Backhendl (Austrian fried chicken) with Styrian potato salad 68

Fried broccoli with anchovies, garlic, chilli and capers 70

Pork schnitzel sandwich with cheese and chilli 72

Spanish-style fried garlic-prawn baguette 74

The fried mushroom burger 76

Spicy smoked tofu burgers 78

## SLOSHED STARCH
—

Authentic smoky chicken burrito 84

Fettuccine with meatballs and cheese 86

Home-made potato gnocchi with a rich ragú 88

Milton's baguette, butter and plum jam pudding 90

Pad Milton 92

Twice-baked potatoes with curry paste, cheese and peas 94

## PLASTERED
## PARTY FOOD
—

Bacon and chive
mini-röstis 100

Baked Camembert with
rosemary and thyme 102

Bruschetta with olives
and anchovies 104

Crostini with tuna and
caper berries 106

English cheese fondue
with perry 108

Steak haché sliders on
toasted brioche 110

## BOOZY
## DESSERTS
—

Crêpes Tom Foster 116

Caramelised rum mango with
vodka lime jelly 118

Milton's tipsy trifle 120

Pannettone with Pedro Ximenez
and ice cream 121

Sherry and ginger log 122

The Big Lebowski sundae 124

## VITTLES
## AND VINE
—

Arnold Bennett omelette with
white Burgundy 130

Curried monkfish and mussels
with Gewürztraminer 132

Salt cod croquettes with
manzanilla 134

Seared scallops, smoked lardons
and black pudding with porter 136

Stuffed grilled mussels with Innis
and Gunn Blonde 138

Venison sausages with cider
sauce and scrumpy 140

All recipes are for two people,
unless otherwise stated. All
recipes call for sea salt and freshly
ground black pepper, to taste,
unless otherwise stated.

Kitchens can be dangerous places
(please see the disclaimer absolving the author
of any responsibility for injury or health
problems that may arise from your efforts).
So these helpful icons indicate some of
the potential risks of injury you may face.

Boiling
water

Grater

Hot
oven / grill

Hot pan

Sharp
knives

In order to try and ensure that you don't
bite off more than you can chew, I have rated each
recipe in terms of the difficulty and/or effort involved
in making it. A recipe may be rated 'difficult' not
because of any particular technical skill that is
required, but simply because there are quite a number
of different processes involved. These ratings make
the assumption that you might be somewhat
impaired in your capacity, but nonetheless you
should be realistic about what you attempt.

[ easy ]     [ moderate ]     [ difficult ]

# THE
# DRUNKEN
# CARNIVORE

—

If alcohol has the capaci
of our most primal lust
why chargrilled meat – a
cavemen – is so promine
barbecue to a man who
will show you his shinies
the barbecued steak an
natural partners for a dr
one and, of course, the
machismo of drinking. H
this kind of über-mascu
more metrosexual kin
gay, bi and transgender
around the fire with t
shoulders and legs of r
grubby hands: cave p

awaken within us some
en perhaps this explains
favoured by all reputable
drunken menus. Show a
had a few beers and he
le. The ubiquitous kebab,
illed chicken seem to be
ng session, or the end of
e part and parcel of the
ever, I personally eschew
. This is an altogether
cookbook: cavewomen,
people should all gather
steaks, and chops and
grasped firmly in their
e of the world, unite!

# CHARGRILLED SMOKY HARISSA CHICKEN

WITH FRIED COUSCOUS
AND HERBS

———

     (fussy)

**FOR THE CHICKEN:** *4 boneless skinless chicken thighs ~ 1 tbsp lemon juice ~ 1 tsp salt ~ 1 tbsp harissa paste ~ 2 tbsp thick Greek yoghurt ~ 1 tsp liquid hickory smoke ~ 1 tbsp olive oil ~ handful of finely chopped fresh mint leaves*
**FOR THE COUSCOUS:** *200g couscous ~ 1 tbsp olive oil ~ 2 onions, halved and thinly sliced ~ 1 tsp cumin ~ good handful of mint, finely chopped ~ good handful of parsley, finely chopped ~ handful of chives, finely chopped ~ few sprigs of oregano, roughly chopped ~ 2 tbsp lemon juice ~ salt, to taste*
**TO SERVE:** *lemon wedges ~ handful of mint leaves, finely chopped*

Harissa is one of my favourite ingredients: unlike many other chilli products it has a delicious deep, unctuous sweetness to it, as well as heat, that immediately conjures, to my mind at least, the southern (i.e. north African) side of the Mediterranean. The couscous, filled with fresh herbs, is a perfect accompaniment.

**Milton's Method** ☞ Place the chicken thighs between 2 pieces of cling film and flatten out a little with a rolling pin to about 0.5–1 centimetre thick.

Prick the chicken thighs with a knife. Place them in a bowl and sprinkle with the lemon juice and salt.

In a separate bowl combine the harissa, yoghurt, liquid hickory smoke, olive oil and mint. Mix well and pour over the chicken.

Place the couscous in a saucepan or measuring jug and pour just enough boiling water over the couscous to cover it. Cover and leave for 10 minutes until the couscous has absorbed all the water.

Heat a frying pan over a medium-high flame and add the olive oil. Cook the onions, stirring regularly, for 8–12 minutes until golden. Add the cumin, stir, then add the couscous. Keep stirring for 3–4 minutes until the couscous has absorbed most of the oil and started to turn golden. Lower the heat, add the herbs, lemon juice and salt, stir again and remove from the heat.

Heat the grill and place the chicken on a wire rack above a baking tray, a few centimetres below the grill. Cook on a high heat until the chicken is golden brown. Turn and cook the other side until it is cooked through, about 10 minutes in total.

Serve with wedges of lemon and a scattering of finely chopped mint leaves.

# CHEAT'S CASSOULET

—

*1 tbsp olive oil ~ 20g butter ~ 4 boneless chicken thighs ~ 4 sausages, chopped into 2–3cm pieces ~ 100g diced streaky bacon/lardons ~ 1 onion, finely chopped ~ 3 cloves garlic, finely chopped ~ 75ml red wine ~ 6 large tomatoes, diced ~ 1 x 400g tin flageolet beans, drained and rinsed ~ 1 tsp finely chopped thyme ~ couple of sprigs of rosemary ~ 250ml chicken stock ~ 2 tsp cornflour ~ 150g very coarse white breadcrumbs ~ salt and pepper, to taste* **TO SERVE:** *frisée lettuce salad*

I remember camping on a small island off the coast of Brittany with a female friend of mine a few years ago and pretty much the only thing on this island was a boulangerie and just about all we had with us was some tins of cassoulet and a little camping stove. We lived off tinned cassoulet and baguettes (and copious amounts of red wine, of course) for about five days, swimming on deserted beaches and circumnavigating our new-found kingdom. It was paradise.

The traditional cassoulet takes a long time to cook, especially with confit duck legs, so I have tried to simplify it somewhat – it is, after all, an uncomplicated, rustic dish that's basically meat with baked beans. This is one-pot cooking at its best.

**Milton's Method** ☞ Heat the oven to 180°C/gas mark 4. Heat the olive oil and butter in a large, heavy casserole dish on a medium-high heat and brown the chicken thighs all over. Take them out and set aside. Add the sausage and bacon to the casserole and cook until golden. Add the onion, cooking and stirring until it becomes translucent, then add the garlic. Add the red wine, let the alcohol evaporate and the liquid reduce, then add the tomatoes, beans, thyme and rosemary.

Stir and mash the tomatoes with the back of
your spoon until they soften and start to
create a thick sauce. Add the stock, season and
bring to the boil. In a separate bowl, mix the
cornflour with a little water and add it to the pan. Stir, turn
down the heat and leave to simmer for 15 minutes with the lid off,
stirring occasionally. The liquid should reduce and thicken further.
Check the seasoning and return the chicken thighs to the casserole,
sprinkle the breadcrumbs over the top and place in the oven.

Leave it to cook for 1.5 hours, or until the breadcrumbs are golden
and form a nice crust. Serve with a frisée lettuce salad.

# CHICKEN LIVERS, BACON AND MUSHROOMS ON TOAST

## WITH CREAMY MUSTARD AND MADEIRA SAUCE

———

*20g butter ~ 1 tbsp olive oil ~ 100g smoked lardons or streaky bacon ~ 40g very finely chopped shallots ~ 200g chestnut mushrooms, cleaned and sliced ~ 400g chicken livers ~ 50ml Madeira wine or medium sherry ~ 1 tbsp wholegrain mustard ~ handful of parsley, finely chopped ~ 100ml double cream ~ 4 slices ciabatta, toasted ~ salt and pepper, to taste*

Chicken livers and mushrooms, with their complementary but entirely different rich, earthy flavours, are two ingredients that seem to go naturally together. I became rather obsessed with mushrooms after I took a house in the New Forest for a while and fell in love with some varieties of fungi that I had never tried before, such as parasols and blewits. For this recipe, though, I am sticking with the regular chestnut mushrooms that can be bought from any supermarket or greengrocers. Call me a philistine, but I prefer my chicken livers just cooked through rather than pink. If you prefer them pink then reduce the cooking time slightly.

**Milton's Method** ☞ Heat the butter and olive oil in a non-stick frying pan over a medium-high heat. When the fat is warm, add the bacon and cook until it has begun to crisp up a little. Add the shallots and sauté for a couple of minutes until they have taken on a little colour. Add the mushrooms and cook for 5 minutes or so, stirring regularly, until they have also taken on some colour and released some of their moisture. Add the livers and cook for a further couple of minutes, then add the Madeira. Allow the alcohol to evaporate and the liquid to reduce for a couple of minutes, then stir in the mustard and half the parsley. Slowly add the cream, and season to taste.

Reduce the heat to medium-low and leave to simmer for 3–4 minutes, stirring occasionally, until the sauce has thickened. Test for seasoning and adjust as required.

Serve on the toasted ciabatta slices with the remaining parsley sprinkled on top, and eat immediately.

# THE PHILLY CHEESESTEAK SANDWICH

—

*2 cloves garlic, crushed or finely chopped ~ 2 tbsp mayonnaise ~ 2 large, soft 'sub' rolls or 1 French baguette ~ 2 tbsp olive oil ~ 1 large onion, halved and thinly sliced ~ 1 green pepper, deseeded and thinly sliced ~ 250g wafer-thin slices of steak ~ 200g provolone, Gouda or Monterey Jack cheese, thinly sliced ~ salt and pepper, to taste*

This is like an all-American doner kebab – thinly shaved fried steak served in a soft roll with cheese, peppers and onion. Yes, a kebab with cheese. It'll feel like you've died and gone to heaven. Some people suggest freezing the steak before you slice it so that you can cut the slices especially thin. I don't consider this necessary.

**Milton's Method** ☞ Combine the garlic and the mayo in a small bowl. Split open your rolls or baguette and spread the mayo inside.

Heat a non-stick frying pan over a moderate heat and add half the olive oil. Add the onion and pepper and sauté for 5–6 minutes until the pepper has softened and the onion has taken on a little colour.

Put the vegetables in a bowl to one side, turn up the heat, add the remaining olive oil to the same pan and then the steak. Season the steak generously with salt and pepper, then stir it with a wooden spatula, pressing down as you go to break down the pieces of beef into smaller bits. Cook until the meat has browned up, just a couple of minutes.

Take the pan off the heat and stir in the onion and pepper. Divide the mixture between your rolls and add the sliced cheese on top. For extra meltedness, pop into a medium oven for a couple of minutes then serve straight away.

# SEARED RARE
# BEEF FILLET

## WITH PARMESAN, ROCKET
## AND AGED BALSAMIC VINEGAR

___

*2 tbsp olive oil ~ 2 tbsp balsamic vinegar ~ 500g beef fillet (thick end) ~ 200g rocket ~ 150g Parmesan or pecorino ~ 100g green olives, pitted and thinly sliced ~ salt and pepper, to taste*

The most important part of this dish is searing the beef properly – this is what will create the delicious, caramelised meat flavour. In order to achieve it, you'll ideally want to have a cast-iron ridged griddle pan that will need about as much heat as you can give it. This level of heat creates its own risks – make sure that only the beef is in contact with the pan and not any part of your own anatomy. This is one for sharing – you'll need a fillet of about 500 grams, which should make enough for 4 people. Try to get a fillet that has some fat marbling in it.

Also, don't stint on the balsamic – cheap, thin vinegar will not help. You will need to splash out a little on this.

**Milton's Method** ☞ Preheat the oven to 220°C/gas mark 7 and get your ridged griddle pan onto the hob over a high heat.
  While the griddle pan is heating up make a dressing from the olive oil and 1 tablespoon of the balsamic and rub this into the fillet. Season with salt and a little freshly ground black pepper and make sure this is massaged into the meat evenly.

Once the griddle pan is very hot, start searing the beef so that it gets nice dark brown char marks all over. This should take 2–3 minutes.

Once the meat has been charred all over, place the fillet in a roasting tray and pop it into the oven – 10 minutes will keep it rare, 12 minutes should be medium-rare, and after 14 minutes it will be increasingly well done. Remove from the oven and leave in the pan to rest for 5 minutes.

Place the rocket on a plate, slice the beef (roughly 1 centimetre-thick slices), then shave the Parmesan on top, drizzle with the remaining balsamic vinegar and garnish with the thinly sliced olives.

# SPICY THAI-STYLE PORK BURGERS

WITH A CUCUMBER
AND PEANUT SALAD

———

**FOR THE BURGERS:** *1 or 2 hot Thai red chillies with seeds, thinly sliced ~ 2 cloves garlic, thinly sliced ~ 1 stick of fresh lemon grass, very thinly sliced ~ handful of coriander (stalks and leaves), roughly chopped ~ 4 lime leaves, thinly sliced ~ 1cm chunk of ginger, finely grated ~ 2 spring onions, thinly chopped ~ 300g seasoned sausage meat ~ 50g streaky bacon, cut into small pieces ~ 1 tbsp soy sauce ~ groundnut or vegetable oil, for frying* **FOR THE CUCUMBER SALAD:** *1 cucumber ~ ½ red onion, very thinly sliced ~ 2 spring onions, thinly sliced ~ 1 red chilli, deseeded and thinly sliced ~ small handful of mint leaves, finely chopped ~ 3 tbsp peanuts, dry-roasted and lightly crushed* **FOR THE SALAD DRESSING:** *½ tsp shrimp paste ~ juice of ½ lime ~ 1 tbsp fish sauce ~ 1 tsp sugar ~ 1 tbsp soy sauce ~ 1 clove garlic, crushed* **TO SERVE:** *white floury bread buns ~ Thai sweet chilli sauce*

This is a great mix of sticky, fatty pork burgers brought to life with chilli, lime leaves, lemon grass and garlic, along with a zingy, refreshing cucumber salad. It's perfect on a hot day with a cold beer when you could put the burgers straight on to the barbecue and serve in a white floury bun with Thai sweet chilli sauce and the salad as a side. The other way of serving these burgers is by mixing some cooled rice noodles with the cucumber salad and popping the burgers on top.

This is at the simple end of the burger scale – because of the amount of pork fat binding everything together, there's very little chance that your burger will fall apart so there's no need to use a binder like eggs. Beware of getting chilli in your eyes.

**Milton's Method** ☞ Whizz the chillies, garlic, lemon grass, coriander, lime leaves, ginger and spring onions together in a food processor until the mixture is very fine and well combined. It should smell fantastic. In a large bowl, combine this mixture with the sausage meat and the bacon. Add the soy sauce and mix everything together very thoroughly. This is best done with your hands. Put the mixture in the fridge so that the pork meat can take on some of the flavour of the aromatic ingredients.

To prepare the salad, first halve the cucumber lengthways, then cut each half lengthways again a few more times, so you have about 6 long strips, then cut these in half lengthways. Combine the cucumber and all the other salad ingredients, except the peanuts, in a large bowl.

Make the dressing by first putting the shrimp paste in a bowl and adding the lime juice. Stir this until it is blended together in a more liquid paste, then add the other ingredients. It will taste rather intense, but don't worry, the water in the cucumber will dilute the dressing somewhat. Adjust the amount of lime juice/sugar to taste. Gently toast the peanuts to release their flavour by dry-frying them for a couple of minutes over a medium heat.

Wet your hands to shape the burgers – there should be enough for 4 good-sized burgers. Heat a splash of groundnut or vegetable oil in a heavy frying pan over a medium-high heat and add the patties once the oil is hot. Cook for about 5 minutes on each side, until the burgers are sticky and golden brown on the outside and cooked through. Add the peanuts and the dressing to the salad and toss well.

Serve immediately in white floury buns with the crunchy cucumber salad and Thai sweet chilli sauce on the side.

# STEAMING
# HOT

—

Curry is a commo
out on the claret. Sp
the befuddled pale
tongues. Sensory ov
effect that we're a
drinks do we go ar
and reflect on life?
mushrooms are for
we want bright lights
action and dancing
and stolen kisses. S
equivalent: bright, b

raving after a night
food blasts through
of our beleaguered
oad is precisely the
– following a few
it quietly by a lake
that's what magic
ter a drink or two
loud conversation,
fumbling romance
food is the culinary
, loud and colourful.

# CALCUTTA-STYLE
# SEEKH KEBAB ROLLS
—

**FOR THE GARNISH:** *½ onion, thinly sliced ~ 2 tbsp lime juice* **FOR THE MINT CHUTNEY:** *2 handfuls of coriander leaves, finely chopped ~ handful of mint leaves, finely chopped ~ 1 tbsp finely grated ginger ~ 1 tbsp finely chopped garlic ~ 1 tsp chopped green chilli ~ 2 tbsp desiccated coconut ~ good pinch of salt ~ 1 tbsp lime juice ~ 50–75ml water* **FOR THE KEBAB:** *250g minced lamb ~ 1 tbsp finely grated ginger ~ 2 cloves garlic, crushed or very finely chopped ~ ½ onion, very finely chopped ~ handful of mint leaves, finely chopped ~ handful of coriander leaves, finely chopped ~ 1 green chilli, deseeded and finely chopped ~ 1 tsp garam masala ~ ½ tsp chilli powder ~ ½ tsp salt ~ 50g melted butter, for basting* **TO SERVE:** *large circular pitta breads* **YOU WILL NEED:** *4 skewers*

There are a number of restaurants around Calcutta's famous New Market like Nizam's and Badshah, that serve a variety of tandoori meat dishes including chicken kathi rolls and mutton rolls. When I was there for a week I got addicted to these places, loving the deep, rich meat flavour imparted by the tandoor alongside the fresh flavours of lime, onion and chilli that are wrapped up alongside them in a thin, fried paratha.

So, this is my take on a seekh kebab roll, with the addition of a mint chutney that is extremely simple to make.

**Milton's Method** ☞ First prepare the garnish. Put the thinly sliced onion in a shallow saucer and marinate with the lime juice. Set aside while you prepare everything else.

Make the mint chutney by putting all the ingredients except the water into a blender (or use a pestle and mortar if you prefer), combining well, then adding enough water to create a thickish paste.

Put all the ingredients for the kebab, apart from the butter, into a large mixing bowl and mix together thoroughly with your hands.

Wet your hands (so that the mixture will not stick to them) and fashion fairly slender sausage shapes about 15 centimetres long around skewers. You should be able to make 4.

Pre-heat the grill on a medium-high heat and place the skewers on a wire rack above a baking tray. Brush the the kebabs with melted butter and place under the grill.

Turn every couple of minutes, basting as you go, until they are lightly browned on all sides and cooked all the way through. This should take about 12 minutes.

Brush one side of the pitta breads with some of the melted butter and place under the grill for a couple of minutes to warm up. Then turn over and warm the other side – you don't want to toast the pittas: they need to stay soft and pliable to wrap around your kebabs.

Serve each kebab on the buttered side of the pitta, dribble over a generous helping of mint chutney, scatter a few slices of onion and wrap into a roll. Eat straight away.

# CHICKEN TIKKA KEBABS

## WITH KEBAB-SHOP SALAD

———

**FOR THE KEBABS:** *400g skinless chicken breasts, cut into 2cm pieces ~ 2 tbsp lemon juice ~ 1 tsp salt ~ 3 tbsp Greek-style natural yoghurt ~ 2 cloves garlic, crushed ~ 2 tsp finely grated ginger ~ ½ tsp bright red paprika ~ ½ tsp cayenne pepper ~ 1 tsp ground cumin ~ pinch of garam masala ~ 25g melted butter, for brushing* **FOR THE SALAD:** *¼ red cabbage, very thinly sliced ~ handful of lettuce, very thinly sliced ~ ½ red onion, halved and very thinly sliced ~ 1 carrot, peeled and finely grated ~ 2 pickled jalapeño peppers (1 per person), roughly chopped ~ ½ cucumber, halved lengthways and thinly sliced ~ 1 large tomato, thinly sliced ~ juice of ½ lemon ~ glug of olive oil ~ handful of parsley, very finely chopped* **TO SERVE:** *warmed pitta breads* **YOU WILL NEED:** *4 skewers*

The kebab is the quintessential accompaniment to a drunken night and the chicken tikka kebab is a personal favourite of mine. Ideally, you should already have the chicken marinating for at least a few hours before you cook, so you could think about doing this before you start drinking so that it (a) tastes better and (b) is really simple to prepare. However, if time is at a premium, the recipe still works with a modest marinating time.

The salad is more Turkish than Indian in origin, I suppose, and this recipe is designed to emulate the typical British kebab-shop salad, with a couple of embellishments. The trick is to make sure that all the ingredients are cut really finely to get that authentic crispy texture.

**Milton's Method** ☞ Put the chicken pieces in a bowl with the lemon juice and salt. Stir or use your hands to make sure all the chicken pieces are well coated. Leave to marinate for 10–15 minutes then add the yoghurt, garlic, ginger, paprika, cayenne pepper, ground cumin and garam masala. Cover and leave to marinate for as long as possible (up to 24 hours). If time is short, then simply pop it in the fridge while you prepare the salad. To make the salad, just throw all the ingredients in a bowl together and mix well.

To cook the chicken, heat your grill so that it is as hot as you can get it. While it's heating up, place the chicken pieces on the skewers and brush with melted butter. Place the skewers on a grill pan, under the grill, and cook so that the edges get a little charred, but the overall effect is lightly browned. This should take around 12–15 minutes in total, turning 2 to 3 times.

Serve with the salad and warmed pitta breads.

# HENRY AND LISA'S MONTSERRAT-STYLE CHICKEN WINGS

*400g chicken wings ~ 1 lemon ~ 5 tsp of all-purpose seasoning, sometimes called 'season-all' ~ 1 tsp paprika ~ 2 tsp allspice (ground pimento) ~ 3 cloves garlic finely chopped ~ 1 large tomato, roughly chopped ~ ½ tbsp fresh thyme or a bit less dry thyme ~ good splash of Worcester sauce ~ 1.5 capfuls malt vinegar ~ 1 chilli, chopped, according to taste ~ small drizzle of olive oil ~ small squeeze of tomato ketchup ~ salt and pepper* **TO SERVE:** *rice or salad*

Henry and Lisa are two of my friends from north London who are used to late nights, serious cooking and waiting for the birds to start singing. Unless they're chickens, that is. In which case, they'll probably already be in Henry and Lisa's oven. Henry's chicken wing recipe has been handed down from his mother who was born in Montserrat.

**Milton's Method** ☞ Pre-heat your oven to 190°C/gas mark 5. Clean the wings with cut segments of lemon, remove any stray feathers, and place the wings on a baking tray. Sprinkle the all-purpose seasoning, paprika, allspice and a little salt and pepper over the wings.

Use your hands to rub the seasoning thoroughly onto the wings then add the rest of the ingredients and massage them in well. Cover the baking tray with foil and bake in the oven for 35 minutes.

Remove the foil and bake for a further 35–40 minutes, taking the tray out a couple of times to give the wings a good shoggling (shaking) so they don't stick to the tray. As they bake, the liquid will evaporate and the wings will develop a rich colour and a delicious crispness.

Serve the wings on their own, or with rice and salad.

'During one of my
treks through
Afghanistan, we lost
our corkscrew.
We were compelled
to live on food and
water for several days.'

W. C. Fields

# PAKISTANI LAMB KOFTA

—

**FOR THE KOFTA:** *300g lamb mince ~ 1 tsp peeled and finely grated ginger ~ ½ small onion, finely chopped ~ 2 green chillies, finely chopped ~ 2 cloves garlic, peeled and finely chopped ~ 1 egg ~ 2 tbsp gram flour (or plain flour) ~ ½ tsp salt ~ ½ tsp garam masala ~ handful of coriander leaves and stalks, finely chopped ~ vegetable or groundnut oil, for frying* **FOR THE SAUCE:** *1 onion, finely chopped ~ 1 bay leaf ~ 1 piece of cinnamon bark ~ 1 tbsp peeled and finely grated ginger ~ 2 cloves garlic, crushed ~ ½ tsp ground turmeric ~ ½ tsp cayenne pepper ~ ½ x 400g tin chopped tomatoes ~ 500ml water ~ salt and pepper* **TO SERVE:** *wide rice noodles ~ handful of coriander leaves, roughly chopped, to garnish*

Pakistani and Bangladeshi meat dishes have been staples of mine ever since a visit to the legendary Tayyabs restaurant on Fieldgate Street in Whitechapel (where Stalin once lived and where Big Ben – the bell – was made).

I prefer eating this best with wide rice noodles, and thinking of it as an Asian version of fettuccine with meatballs.

**Milton's Method** ☞ Combine all the ingredients for the kofta in a large bowl and mix well with your hands. Wet your hands and make individual balls about the size of small plums. Put these on a plate and set aside while you make the sauce.

Heat some vegetable or groundnut oil in a large non-stick saucepan and add the onion, bay leaf and cinnamon. Cook on a medium-high heat until the onion is golden.

Add the ginger and garlic, stir and cook for a minute, add the spices, stir and cook for 10 seconds, then add the tomatoes and seasoning.

Cook for about 5 minutes to allow some of the liquid to evaporate, stirring occasionally. Add the water, bring to the boil and simmer for a few minutes to reduce again, then gently add the meatballs to sauce. Cover the pan, place on a low heat, and leave to simmer for around 15–20 minutes.

Serve with wide rice noodles tossed in butter and garnish with chopped coriander leaves.

# CHARGRILLED VEGETABLE AND CHEESE QUESADILLA

WITH FRIED EGG

---

*1 tbsp olive oil ~ ½ tsp salt ~ 1 red pepper, deseeded and thinly sliced ~ 8 cherry tomatoes ~ 4 corn tortillas ~ 150g extra mature cheddar, grated ~ 4 spring onions, very finely shredded ~ 1 jalapeño pepper, finely chopped ~ 1 tsp dried oregano ~ freshly ground black pepper ~ 2 free range eggs ~ olive oil, for frying* **TO SERVE:** *chipotle sauce ~ lime wedges ~ Greek yoghurt or sour cream*

The first time I tried this recipe I used eggs bought at the roadside from a house in the middle of nowhere. When I opened the box, I discovered beautiful pale pastel-blue eggs, marked with their laid-on date in a neat, pencilled hand. Cracking the thin blue shells revealed boisterous, large orange yolks that made the best fried eggs I had ever tasted. Even more delicious when placed on a quesadilla filled with cheese and tomatoes and peppers that have been deliberately slightly burnt a little to give them a smoky flavour. You can use oil to fry your quesadilla but I prefer to dry fry mine – this recipe has plenty of fat going on already.

**Milton's Method** ☞ Heat the grill as hot as you can get it. Pour the olive oil and salt into a small bowl and add the pepper and tomatoes. Mix to cover well with oil then place them on a baking tray under the grill, fairly close to the heat. You want the skins to blacken a little – there's plenty of juice so they won't burn to a crisp too easily. Once you've got the smell of a little smoke, turn everything over and cook the other side – this should take around 5–6 minutes.

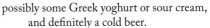

Place one tortilla in a frying pan of the same size. Evenly spread the cheese, spring onions, tomatoes, pepper, jalapeño and oregano and season with black pepper but no salt.

Place another tortilla on top and gently press it down. Cook on a medium-high heat until the bottom tortilla has become toasted and golden (about 2–3 minutes) then place a plate over the top of the frying pan, flip the quesadilla out onto the plate and return to the pan to cook the other side, again for around 2–3 minutes.

Repeat (for the second quesadilla), set aside and fry your eggs. I prefer to do this in olive oil over a low to medium heat so that the white stays soft. Cut the quesadillas into triangles and serve each with an egg on top, a squeeze of lime, plenty of chipotle sauce, possibly some Greek yoghurt or sour cream, and definitely a cold beer.

# QUICK COUSCOUS
# CHICKEN BIRYANI

—

*2 skinless boneless chicken breasts and thighs, cut into 2cm chunks ~ 1 tsp cayenne pepper ~ 1 tsp red paprika ~ ½ tsp turmeric ~ 2 tsp ground coriander ~ 1 tsp curry powder ~ 1 tsp salt ~ ½ tsp powdered garlic ~ 400ml chicken stock ~ large pinch of saffron ~ 25g butter ~ 1 tbsp vegetable oil ~ 2 onions, thinly sliced into half rings ~ 2 bay leaves ~ 4 whole cloves ~ 1 small stick of cinnamon ~ 3 cardamom pods ~ 200g couscous ~ 250g potatoes, cut into 2–3cm chunks and boiled until just cooked ~ 75g frozen peas* **TO SERVE:** *cucumber raita ~ poppadums*

In Karnataka, and Kerala in particular (the best was in Kannur, Kerala), I ate biryani all the time, most often goat biryani that I quickly learnt to eat with my right hand off large banana leaves. Crisp poppadums are served with the meal and provide a great textural contrast. The tender meat and fragrant rice is wonderful, but it is something that generally takes a long time to cook. I decided create a shorter, easier version.

It does not pretend to be comparable to a 'proper' biryani, and purists will certainly scoff, but it is extraordinarily quick and easy to prepare and is still very tasty.

**Milton's Method** ☞ Place the chicken pieces in a large bowl and add the cayenne pepper, paprika, turmeric, coriander, curry powder, salt and powdered garlic. Make sure each piece of chicken is well coated with the spice mix. Heat your stock (or make it up, if you're using a cube), and add the saffron. Leave to stand.

In a heavy frying pan, heat the butter and the oil on a medium-high flame. There is quite a lot of fat, but this is important to keep the chicken tender and the couscous buttery. Once the butter has melted and is bubbling a little, add the chicken pieces and cook until coloured slightly on all sides. They should not be cooked through. This will take just 3–4 minutes. Using a slotted spoon, remove the chicken pieces and set aside.

Using the same fat and the same pan, add the onion, bay leaves, cloves, cinnamon, cardamom and a good pinch of salt and cook the onions for around 12 minutes, stirring regularly until the onions are richly coloured but not burnt.

Add the dried couscous, stir, then add the chicken, boiled potato pieces and frozen peas. Finally, add the stock, stir well, cover and turn the heat down to very low. Keep on the heat for 5 minutes then kill the flame completely but leave the lid on for a further 10 minutes to give the opportunity for the flavours to infuse and the chicken to cook through.

Serve immediately with cucumber raita and as many poppadums as you can get your hands on.

# WELL-OILED

—

Fried food is just as ubiq
hedonistic night as losing ca
waking up in the morning w
But frying can be dangerous
serve as a cautionary tale. A
going home and cooking sor
an area of London where Tu
of fruit, vegetables and ch
I picked up my nuts and hea
No. In my drunken wisdom
wok. I whacked the heat on hi
got a beer and went and sa
think about the wok or the c
sounded like small arms fire
the sound of chestnuts expl
the kitchen walls. There is s
the unctuousness that fryi
evenly across the palate. Ju

s an accompaniment to a
wn the back of taxi seats or
ur shoes and socks still on.
of my frying stories should
night out, at 4am I fancied
estnuts. I lived at the time in
grocers sell a fantastic array
ts, twenty-four hours a day.
home. Would I roast them?
cided to fry them in oil in a
t in the oil and the chestnuts,
the living room and did not
nuts again until I heard what
ng from the kitchen. It was
g and spattering oil all over
hing deeply satisfying about
parts, with flavour spread
n't kill yourself making it.

# BACKHENDL (AUSTRIAN FRIED CHICKEN)

## WITH STYRIAN POTATO SALAD

———

**FOR THE POTATO SALAD:** *500g waxy potatoes ~ 100ml vegetable stock, home-made or bought ~ 50ml pumpkin seed oil (or extra virgin olive oil) ~ 50ml cider vinegar ~ 1 onion, finely diced ~ 2 tbsp pumpkin seeds ~ handful of chives, finely chopped ~ salt and freshly ground black pepper* **FOR THE CHICKEN:** *2 chicken breasts, 2 drumsticks and 2 thighs, skin removed ~ 100g flour ~ 1 tsp onion powder ~ 1 tsp garlic powder ~ 2 tsp salt ~ 1 tsp black pepper ~ 3 eggs, beaten ~ 150g fine breadcrumbs ~ vegetable oil, for frying*

According to my Austrian friends there are only two KFCs in the whole of Austria – both in Vienna. This dish probably explains why. It is fried chicken, Austrian style, and in Austria it is usually served with a potato salad.

My difficulty with this recipe is that the chicken should be deep-fried but, in an effort to spare you, my dear readers, from an ignominious end, here I have decided to shallow-fry and then bake the chicken, which I think gives equally good results.

Delicious pumpkin seed oil is a common, though still expensive, commodity in Austria. If you cannot find it, try using good quality olive oil instead.

**Milton's Method** ☞ Put the potatoes, whole and with their skins, into a large saucepan of cold water. Bring to the boil and cook for around 20 minutes until cooked through, but not mushy. Drain and set aside to cool a little.

To make the dressing, mix the vegetable stock, pumpkin seed oil, cider vinegar, onion and salt and black pepper to taste, together in a small bowl. Stir well.

Peel and slice the potatoes and place in a large bowl then pour the dressing over them. Set aside to allow the potatoes to absorb the dressing. Toast the pumpkin seeds and add them as garnish along with the chopped chives.

To cook the chicken, preheat the oven to 180C⁰/gas mark 4. In a large bowl, add the flour, onion powder, garlic powder, salt and pepper and mix well to combine. Beat the eggs in a shallow bowl and place the breadcrumbs in another. Coat the chicken pieces in the flour, then dip them in the egg and finally in the breadcrumbs. Make sure each piece is well coated. Put on a plate, ready to cook.

Place a large heavy frying pan over a medium heat and add vegetable oil to about 1.5-centimetre depth. Once the oil is hot, place the chicken pieces in the pan. Be careful of spitting oil. Cook on each side until the breadcrumbs are crisp and golden (around 7–8 minutes) then drain and place on a baking tray lined with grease-proof paper. Place in the oven for about 15–20 minutes or until the chicken is cooked through.

Serve with the potato salad.

# FRIED BROCCOLI

WITH ANCHOVIES, GARLIC,
CHILLI AND CHILLI AND CAPERS

———

*1 tbsp groundnut or vegetable oil ~ 25g tinned anchovies, finely chopped ~*
*2 cloves garlic, finely chopped ~ 2 red chillies, thinly sliced ~ 1 large head of broccoli,*
*washed and cut into small florets ~ 1 tbsp capers ~ 2 tbsp pumpkin seeds*

You can eat this as a side dish or combine it with some pasta and
some torn buffalo mozzarella to make a more substantial meal.
The anchovies and capers provide all the salt you need – don't add
any more.

**Milton's Method** ☞ In a large frying pan or wok, heat the oil over
a high flame and add the anchovies, garlic and chillies. Cook for
about 2 minutes, stirring constantly and crushing the anchovies with
the back of your spoon. Make sure the garlic does not burn.

Add the broccoli and the capers, stir well and cook for about 5
minutes, until the broccoli has coloured slightly but is still firm and
crunchy. In a separate pan, dry-toast the
pumpkin seeds until they are light brown
and crunchy.

Serve the broccoli sprinkled with
the pumpkin seeds.

'Never despise a drink
because it is easy
to make and/or uses
commercial mixes.
Unquestioning devotion
to authenticity is,
in any department of
life, a mark of the naive
– or worse.'

Kingsley Amis

# PORK SCHNITZEL SANDWICH

## WITH CHEESE AND CHILLI AND A WATERCRESS SALAD

*2 pork loin steaks, each about 150g ~ 100g plain flour ~ 75g finely grated Parmesan ~ handful of thyme, finely chopped ~ 1 tsp chilli flakes ~ 150g fine white breadcrumbs ~ 2 eggs, beaten ~ vegetable oil, for frying ~ salt and pepper* **TO SERVE:** *2 white crusty rolls (if you can get hold of them: 'Kaiser rolls') ~ 50g watercress ~ 1 tbsp lemon juice ~ 1 tbsp olive oil*

The Austrians have much to teach the rest of the world on the subject of drinking and the food required to accompany it. Believe me: I know. During one debauched evening at a southern Austrian buschenschank – a kind of rural wine tavern where the wine is produced at the tavern's own vineyard and food is sourced locally – we were served roughly six bottles of wine per person and a meaty banquet that included rye bread with warm beef dripping, pork dripping, roast pork, various charcuterie, chicken liver pâté, sheep's cheese and slices of beef in jelly with garnishes and condiments including gherkins, grated horseradish and mustard.

This dish takes its inspiration from the Austrian countryside with a nod to Vienna and the schnitzelsemmel – a sandwich where the primary ingredient is one of Austria's most famous exports: the schnitzel, sometimes made from veal, but often pork as well. In Austria, this is usually made with a Kaiser roll, but any kind of white crusty roll will do.

**Milton's Method** ☞ Flatten the steaks between 2 pieces of cling film with a rolling pin, so that they're about 0.5-centimetre thick.

Season the flour generously with salt and pepper in a shallow bowl Combine the Parmesan, chopped thyme, chilli flakes and breadcrumbs and place in a separate shallow bowl.

Coat the pork with the flour, then dredge through the beaten egg and cover in the breadcrumb mix. Make sure that the meat is evenly and generously coated. Repeat with the other steak. Ideally, leave in the fridge for at least 10 minutes to let the breadcrumbs stick. Shallow-fry in a little vegetable oil on a medium-high heat until both sides are crisp and golden.

Serve in the rolls with the watercress
drizzled with the lemon juice
and a little olive oil.

# SPANISH-STYLE FRIED GARLIC-PRAWN BAGUETTE

---

*2 large tomatoes, finely diced ~ 75ml good quality extra virgin olive oil ~ 4 large cloves garlic, crushed and very finely chopped ~ 2 tsp paprika flakes ~ 8 very large prawns, uncooked, with shells (4 per person) ~ 1 tsp sweet paprika ~ 50ml brandy ~ 1 lemon (½ juiced, ½ cut into 2 wedges) ~ handful of parsley, finely chopped ~ 1 fresh white baguette ~ salt*

Ah, those many hours I have whiled away drinking sherry and cava and eating garlicky prawns, patatas bravas, tortilla Española and the like, have been some of the happiest of my life. This is an extremely quick and simple recipe to prepare and perfect for a summer drinking snack with cold beer or a fresh white wine.

**Milton's Method** ☞ First make the tomato salsa. In a small bowl, add the tomatoes, a glug of the olive oil and one of the cloves of garlic and season generously with salt, pepper and a pinch of paprika flakes. Mix thoroughly and set aside to allow the flavours to mingle.

Warm the remaining olive oil in a frying pan over a medium-high heat, then add the rest of the garlic and cook for about 30 seconds. Be careful not to burn it. Add the prawns, the remaining paprika flakes and the sweet paprika. Stir. The prawns should be pinkening already. Add the brandy (careful – there may be a quick burst of flame) and then the lemon juice. Add the chopped parsley and a little salt, swirl the pan and, when they're pink on the bottom, flip the prawns over to cook the other side. They should need no more than about 4 minutes in total. When pink all over, remove the prawns from the pan and set them aside. Take the pan off the heat and reserve the cooking sauce.

Divide the baguette between 2 plates and slice lengthways, peel the prawns and place in the baguette halves. This is a messy business that you can make the most of by licking your fingers frequently. Spoon some of the cooking liquor over them, then the tomato salsa and finish with a squeeze of lemon. Garnish with the lemon wedges.

Tuck in.

# THE FRIED
# MUSHROOM BURGER
—

*50g plain flour ~ 1 tsp salt and some freshly ground black pepper ~ handful of finely chopped chives ~ 2 Portobello mushroom caps (1 per person), 2 parasol caps (1 per person) or 4 x 2cm thick slices of giant puffball (2 per person) ~ 4 rashers smoked streaky bacon* **FOR THE FRENCH DRESSING:** *1 tsp Dijon mustard ~ ½ clove garlic ~ 1 tbsp white wine vinegar ~ 4 tbsp olive oil ~ salt and pepper, to taste* **TO SERVE:** *2 soft white baps ~ handful of salad leaves*

There are a few different options with this mushroom burger, but of varying degrees of practicality. The easiest type of mushroom to get hold of is a Portobello (readily available in most greengrocers and supermarkets), but it's worth trying this recipe with a couple of more exotic types of fungi. The tastiest is the parasol, the most fun is the giant puffball. All three are large mushrooms and all you will need to do is to cook 1 or 2 pieces per person to rustle up a satisfying meal.

If you'd prefer to keep it vegetarian, dispense with the bacon and add a little more fat to your pan.

If you are picking wild mushrooms, make sure you know what you're doing – some types of mushroom can be lethal. But the giant puffball is one that you cannot mistake – if you see something the size and shape of a football and it's not a football, then it's probably a giant puffball.

**Milton's Method** ☞ Season the flour with a teaspoon of salt, a few grinds of black pepper, and the finely chopped chives.

Dampen each piece of mushroom very slightly with some water and dip in the flour so that it is thinly coated all over.

Combine all the ingredients for the French dressing. Add a little oil to a heavy frying pan and heat over a medium flame. Add the bacon and cook until crisp. Remove the bacon and keep warm.

Add the floured mushrooms to the pan and cook, turning once, until the flour is crispy and golden on the outside. This should take a matter of minutes. Place the mushrooms in the soft buns with the bacon. Add salad leaves on top and spoon a generous amount of dressing over the top.

Eat immediately.

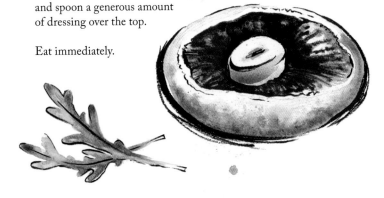

# SPICY SMOKED TOFU BURGERS

## WITH CORIANDER ROAST SQUASH AND AVOCADO PURÉE

———

   toil

**FOR THE TOFU BURGERS:** *1 onion, roughly chopped ~ 1 clove garlic, chopped ~ 1 chilli, chopped ~ 1 medium carrot, peeled and finely grated ~ 200g tinned red kidney beans ~ 150g firm smoked tofu, drained ~ 1 tsp sweet paprika ~ 1 tsp coriander powder ~ 1 tbsp sesame seeds ~ handful of flat-leaf parsley, finely chopped ~ 2 tsp vegetable stock powder ~ 2 tsp cornflour ~ 1 egg, beaten* **FOR THE CORIANDER ROAST SQUASH:** *1 butternut squash, peeled and roughly chopped ~ 2 tbsp olive oil ~ 1 tbsp lightly crushed coriander seeds ~ 2 cloves garlic, crushed ~ 2 dried bird's eye chillies, crushed ~ ½ tsp salt ~ freshly ground black pepper* **FOR THE AVOCADO PURÉE:** *2 ripe avocados ~ 2 spring onions, finely chopped ~ good pinch of sea salt ~ glug of extra virgin olive oil ~ 2 tbsp water* **TO SERVE:** *burger buns*

You may (or may not) think of tofu as a dreary, insipid abomination that only has relevance if you are interested in saving the rainforests and hundreds of thousands of cattle from being slaughtered in hideously inhumane ways. And these are both laudable aims that I think are well worth pursuing. But for the sceptical amongst you, I'd also like to urge you to rethink your dislike of this much-maligned product by trying this recipe that is quite expressly a 'tofu dish for people who don't like tofu'.

Smoked tofu is available in many different flavours and strengths; the strongest can be extremely intense – salty, dense and smoky, with a consistency like a semi-hard cheese. The most important thing is to make sure that the tofu is firm, as a too-soggy tofu will result in sad and sloppy burgers.

This can be a vegan recipe if you exclude the egg, but including it will help your burgers to bind together more effectively.

**Milton's Method** ☞ Preheat your oven to 220°C/gas mark 7. Line a baking tray with greaseproof paper. Whack all the burger ingredients in a food processor and blitz for a few seconds to form a rough paste; it's good to retain a bit of texture. If you don't have a food processor, use a potato masher to get the consistency right.

Form the mixture into 4 burgers with wet hands and place on the baking paper. At the same time prepare the squash by mixing it with all the other ingredients and placing in the oven in a hot baking tray.

Bake the burgers for about 35–40 minutes until light golden brown. The squash should take the same amount of time. While the burgers and squash are in the oven, make the avocado purée by mashing the avocado flesh with the back of a fork then combining with the other ingredients to make a creamy purée.

Remove the burgers from the oven and leave to rest for a couple of minutes. This will help them to set.

Serve in buns, or on their own, with the purée and squash.

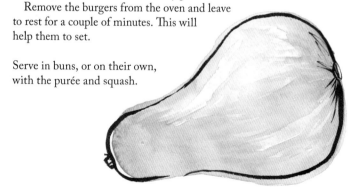

# SLOSHED
# STARCH

—

Alcohol may be calorific
in a pint of beer or a
drinking nonetheless ten
You'll quite likely need
your hands on if you're
of partying and possib
best way to soak up the
kind of purposeful ener
the night, is to eat carl
of starchy carbs, despi
recently received from
Without pasta, bread, p
know how I would m
Well, I guess I'd still
Now, if I didn't have th

roximately 200 calories
ium glass of wine), but
make us even hungrier.
e calories you can get
ning on a vigorous night
en after-partying. The
ze, and to give you the
keep you going through
drates. I am a big lover
e bad press they have
protein-loving media.
es and noodles I don't
it through the week.
fine wine and cheese.
I really would struggle.

# AUTHENTIC, SMOKY CHICKEN BURRITO

 toil

*4 chicken breasts, skinless and boneless* **FOR THE MARINADE:** *4 cloves garlic, peeled and roughly chopped ~ 1 red onion, peeled and roughly chopped ~ 2 regular green chillies, chopped ~ 2 tsp cumin ~ 2 tsp dried oregano ~ 1 tbsp lime juice ~ 1 tsp sugar ~ 2 tsp salt ~ freshly ground black pepper* **FOR THE RICE:** *100g long grain rice ~ large handful of coriander, chopped ~ juice of 1 lime ~ ½ tsp salt* **FOR THE BEANS:** *1 tbsp olive oil ~ 1 small onion, chopped ~ 1 clove garlic, crushed and finely chopped ~ 1 tinned chipotle pepper (soft), chopped ~ 1 tsp cumin ~ 1 x 300g tin pinto beans, washed and drained ~ 100ml chicken stock ~ 1 tsp cornflour ~ salt and pepper* **TO SERVE:** *flour tortillas ~ red chilli sauce ~ grated cheddar cheese ~ sour cream*

The chicken really does need time to marinate for this recipe, and it's best if you prepare it the night before to cook the following evening. This is a meal in itself and needs no accompaniment but a cold beer. The great chicken flavour is mainly due to the chipotle marinade and the Maillard reaction that you get from cooking.

**Milton's Method** ☞ For the chicken marinade, combine all the ingredients in a blender, and blitz. Prick the chicken pieces with a sharp knife and place in an airtight container or sealable sandwich bag with the marinade. Leave to marinate in the fridge for 12–24 hours. Prepare the rice by following the packet instructions. When cooked, add the coriander, lime juice and salt. Set aside and keep warm.

For the beans, heat the olive oil in a non-stick saucepan over a medium heat and add the onion. Cook, stirring occasionally, until softened, then add the garlic, chilli and cumin. Cook for a further

minute or two then add the beans and the stock and season well. Bring to the boil and simmer for 5 minutes. Mix the cornflour with a little water and add to the pan. Stir until the sauce has thickened a little and become slightly glutinous. Set aside and keep warm.

To cook the chicken, heat a heavy griddle pan or a George Foreman Grill to high then add the chicken, pressing it down to sear and caramelise the surface. Once the chicken has got pronounced sear marks on one side, turn to cook the other side. This should take about 8–10 minutes in total. Turn off the heat and leave to rest and cook through in the pan for 2–3 minutes.

Heat the tortillas, following the packet instructions, add a generous serving of rice and beans to the middle of each. Cut the chicken into 2-centimetre cubes and place on top, and add chilli sauce, cheese and sour cream to taste.

Roll into wraps and eat straight away.

# FETTUCCINE
# WITH MEATBALLS
# AND CHEESE
—

**FOR THE MEATBALLS:** *200g minced beef ~ 100g pork sausagemeat ~ 2 cloves garlic, finely chopped ~ 1 egg ~ 1 tbsp Parmesan ~ 2 tbsp breadcrumbs ~ 1 tbsp dried oregano ~ handful of parsley, finely chopped ~ freshly ground black pepper ~ ½ tsp salt* **FOR THE TOMATO SAUCE:** *2 tbsp olive oil ~ ½ onion, very finely chopped ~ 2 cloves garlic, crushed or finely chopped ~ 1 red chilli, deseeded and finely chopped ~ ½ tsp chilli flakes ~ 1 tbsp dried oregano ~ 75ml red wine ~ 1 tbsp balsamic vinegar ~ 1 x 400g tin chopped tomatoes ~ ½ tsp sugar ~ grated zest of ½ lemon ~ 100ml water ~ salt and pepper, to taste* **TO SERVE:** *200g dried fettuccine ~ 75g grated Parmesan*

Okay, so cooking meatballs is a mainstay of gangster films; but put away the attitude and the razor blades for slicing the garlic. Right now. Who do you think you are? Some kind of wise guy?

Fine. Let's begin. Are we making our own pasta here? Of course we're not. Who do you think I am? Jamie frickin' Oliver? Antonio bleedin' Carluccio? No. Go to the shop to buy your pasta. Fettuccine is best with meatballs. All you have to do is make the meatballs, cook a simple tomato sauce and grate a bunch of cheese on top. Semplice! (Simple) Perfetto! (Perfect).

**Milton's Method** ☞ Combine all the ingredients for the meatballs in a large bowl and mix well – use a spoon if you prefer, but hands are best. With wet hands, divide the mixture up into small balls the size of walnuts – you should end up with about a dozen. Put them on a plate, cover with some cling film and place in the fridge until needed.

For the sauce, put a frying pan on a medium heat, add the olive oil and fry the onion for 5–6 minutes, stirring frequently, until softened and just beginning to turn gold. Add the garlic, chilli and oregano, cook for about a minute, then add the wine. Be careful – the pan will spit.

Turn up the heat, bring to the boil and reduce the liquid by half, stirring, then add the balsamic vinegar. Simmer for another couple of minutes then add the tinned tomatoes, sugar, lemon zest and water. Season generously. Stir well, bring to the boil and simmer over a low heat for 10 minutes

Place the meatballs in the tomato sauce and cook on a low heat for 15–20 minutes, turning occasionally so that they get cooked through. Cook the fettuccine according to the packet instructions.

Serve the meatballs in their sauce with the fettuccine and a generous grating of Parmesan.

# HOME-MADE
# POTATO GNOCCHI

WITH A RICH RAGÚ

—

**FOR THE RAGÚ** *3 tbsp olive oil ~ 1 red onion, diced ~ 2 stalks celery, diced ~ 1 carrot, diced ~ 2 bay leaves ~ 100g streaky bacon, roughly chopped ~ 250g minced beef ~ 100g chicken livers, trimmed, washed and finely chopped ~ 250ml red wine ~ 1 x 400g tin chopped tomatoes ~ 50g tomato purée ~ 1 tsp grated nutmeg ~ salt and pepper* **FOR THE GNOCCHI:** *350g cold mashed potato ~ 250g flour (and extra for dusting) ~ 1 egg, beaten ~ salt and pepper*

One of my Italian friends tells the story of how, as a child, when she used to get out of bed in the morning and go down to the kitchen, her mother would already be cooking the ragú for the evening meal. As it was bubbling away, her mother would poach an egg or two in the sauce and serve it with some bread for breakfast and carry on cooking.

While most of the recipes I have included in this cookbook have been designed with instant gratification in mind, this is one best suited to a Sunday afternoon, perhaps, where it would be wise to sit back and open a bottle or two of red and wait for your ragú to simmer, mature and thicken.

**Milton's Method** ☞ In a large, heavy casserole dish, heat the olive oil over a medium heat and add the onion, celery, carrot and bay leaves. Cook for about 10 minutes, stirring now and again, then add the bacon. Turn the heat up and allow the bacon to colour slightly before browning the beef and adding the chicken livers. Once all the meat is well browned, add the wine, tomatoes, tomato purée, nutmeg and seasoning. Stir well, bring to the boil and turn the heat down to low. Simmer for 2 hours, stirring occasionally to stop the sauce from sticking. Add a little water if it does.

To prepare the gnocchi, combine the mashed potato, flour and a beaten egg, along with some seasoning, in a large bowl and knead together to make a dough. Roll this into a ball, then take chunks from the bowl and roll them, with a little extra flour to prevent sticking, into long worms about 0.5 centimetres thick. Cut into 1.5-centimetre lengths and place on a plate dusted with a little more flour.

When the ragú is ready, bring a large pan of salted water to the boil and drop in the gnocchi. Once they bob to the top, after 3–4 minutes, they are ready. Remove from the pan with a slotted spoon. Serve immediately with a generous helping of ragú.

# MILTON'S BAGUETTE, BUTTER AND PLUM JAM PUDDING

    ( fussy )

*1 slightly stale baguette, thinly sliced ~ 50g butter (and extra for greasing) ~ 5 tbsp plum jam ~ 50g sultanas ~ 2 large eggs ~ 2 large egg yolks ~ 40g caster sugar ~ 1 vanilla pod, halved ~ 300ml double cream ~ 300ml full fat milk ~ 75ml French brandy ~ 2 tbsp soft brown sugar* **TO SERVE:** *cream or vanilla ice cream*

This gloriously indulgent pudding is packed full of calorific treats (like most of the best desserts are).

**Milton's Method** ☞ Preheat your oven to 180°C/gas mark 4. Grease a small, shallow, rectangular baking dish. Spread butter and jam on both sides of your sliced baguette and place the slices in overlapping layers in the dish, adding the sultanas as you go.

Make a basic custard by beating the eggs, egg yolks and caster sugar in a mixing bowl until they are creamy, then scrape the seeds from the vanilla pod into the mixture. Beat in the cream, milk and the brandy. Pour the mixture over the bread slices in the baking dish and leave for 20 minutes so the bread can soak it all up. Sprinkle the soft brown sugar on top.

Place the baking dish in a roasting tin and pour boiling water around the outside – you are basically creating a bain-marie type arrangement so that the pudding poaches rather than roasts. Place in the oven and bake for about 45 minutes until golden on top.

Remove from the oven and leave to rest for 10 minutes. While it's resting, glaze the top with the remaining plum jam, loosened with a couple of teaspoons of hot water.

Serve with fresh cream or vanilla ice cream.

'I don't believe in
dining on an
empty stomach.'

W.C. Fields

# PAD MILTON

*150g dried ho fun rice noodles ~ 100g firm tofu, cut into 2 x 1cm strips ~ 2–3 tbsp vegetable or groundnut oil ~ 4 spring onions, finely shredded, dividing the white and green parts ~ 3 cloves garlic, crushed ~ 200g uncooked, shelled and deveined large prawns ~ 2 eggs, beaten ~ 50g bean sprouts ~ 3 tbsp fish sauce (nam pla) ~ 2 tbsp lime juice ~ 1 tbsp brown sugar ~ 2 tbsp tamarind paste ~ ½ tsp dried hot chilli flakes ~ 2 tbsp freshly toasted and lightly crushed peanuts ~ ground white pepper* **TO SERVE:** *lime wedges*

This is my take on the classic Thai-style Pad Thai. The secret is in getting the balance right between sweet (from the sugar), sour (from the lime juice and tamarind), salty (from the fish sauce) and spicy (from the chilli). Of all the Pad Thai dishes I ever ate in Thailand, only one really disappointed. It was made with stringy, instant-style noodles. It's important to use dried rice noodles and I prefer the wide, 'ho-fun' style. Don't be put off by the long list of ingredients – the only effort required is in taking them out of the cupboard as the cooking itself is a cinch and so quick.

**Milton's Method** ☞ Soak the noodles in hot water, following the packet instructions. Pat the tofu dry with tissue paper. Heat a wok over a strong flame and add 2 tablespoons of oil. Stir-fry the tofu until it starts to brown, then add the white part of the spring onion and the garlic and continue to stir-fry.

Meanwhile, when the noodles are softened but still have a little firmness, drain them and, while they are still in the colander, pour a little oil over them and run your fingers through the noodles with the oil to stop them from sticking together.

Add the prawns to the wok, cook until just pinkening slightly, then add the noodles and stir well.

Move the noodles and prawns to one side of the wok and add the beaten egg to the other. Cook without stirring until the egg is loosely set – 30 seconds or so – then break up and mix well with the noodles. Then in succession add the bean sprouts, green part of the spring onions, fish sauce, lime juice, brown sugar, tamarind paste and chilli flakes, stirring and tossing the contents of the wok until well combined and the noodles are tender. Season with white pepper.

Serve immediately with peanuts scattered over each serving and a wedge of lime on the side.

# TWICE-BAKED POTATOES

WITH CURRY PASTE,
CHEESE AND PEAS

———

*2 large baking potatoes ~ 1 onion, halved and thinly sliced ~ 1 tbsp olive oil ~ 50g butter ~ 150g extra mature cheddar, grated ~ 2 tbsp Patak's balti curry paste ~ 75g frozen peas ~ 1 tbsp lemon juice ~ handful of finely chopped chives ~ salt and pepper* **TO SERVE:** *1 red chilli, finely sliced ~ Greek yoghurt ~ green salad*

This is an old classic of mine that is surprisingly delicious and could not be easier to make. The one downside is that you'll have to wait for your potatoes to bake. You can, of course, take a shortcut by using the microwave, but you won't get the great flavour from the skin that baking in the oven gives.

**Milton's Method** ☞ Preheat your oven to 220°C/gas mark 7. Bake the potatoes. I normally do this by pricking the potatoes with a fork a few times and putting them straight into the oven. No oil. No salt. No nuffink. They should take 45–60 minutes to cook. While the potatoes are cooking, fry the sliced onion in a little olive oil over a medium-high heat until they have taken on a little colour. Set aside.

You want the skin of your potatoes crispy and the flesh soft and fluffy. Check by running a skewer through the potato. If it runs through cleanly then it's done.

Take the potatoes out and cut in half length-ways. Scoop the soft flesh into a large bowl and add the other ingredients: the butter, cheese, fried onions, curry paste, frozen peas, lemon juice, salt and pepper and half of the chives. Mix well then cram back into the potato shells. Return to the oven, and bake for another 15 minutes until crispy on top.

Serve with some red chilli and chives sprinkled on top, some Greek yoghurt alongside, and a crisp green salad.

# PLASTERED
# PARTY
# FOOD

—

Eating and drinking with
pleasures, but cooking for t
time often isn't. People say
best people hang out at pa
know this maxim, the higher
overall 'good people quotie
sure I want people around n
a dish. For me it's a matter
on producing food, it is ha
Not everyone is the same —
one knows at least one), for
something together while i
their sharp wit, amazing s
annoying superhuman-ness
same way that I do. This ch
dishes that are quick and
also fun and delicious to e
(perhaps), while also lea

ds is one of life's great
while trying to have a good
the kitchen is where all the
but the more people that
ikelihood that the kitchen's
ill be reduced. And I'm not
en I'm still trying to concoct
ncentration; if I am focused
me to focus on my guests.
e perfect hostesses (every-
nce, who effortlessly throw
ssing all around them with
of humour and generally
't seem to struggle in the
, then, gives a few ideas for
to prepare, but which are
aking you look superhuman
you to enjoy the party.

# BACON AND CHIVE
# MINI-RÖSTIS

—

     (fussy)

(makes approximately 24 rösti) *900g potatoes ~ 3 tbsp olive oil ~ 250g smoked lardons in tiny dice ~ 2 onions, grated ~ 1 tsp salt ~ 1 tsp freshly ground black pepper ~ 2 large handfuls of chives, finely chopped ~ butter, for greasing* **TO SERVE:** *sour cream*

These are perfect little snacks to serve up at a party. You will ideally need a couple of mini-tart trays (each for a dozen tarts) to cook your röstis in, though otherwise, you can shape them and cook them on a baking tray instead.

**Milton's Method** ☞ Parboil the potatoes whole in a large saucepan of water for 10–12 minutes until they are slightly cooked but still firm. Leave them in the fridge to cool.

Add a little olive oil to a frying pan and cook the diced lardons until just starting to golden. Drain and set aside on kitchen paper. Preheat your oven to 230°C/gas mark 8.

Once the potatoes have cooled, peel them and grate them into a large bowl. Add the cooked lardons, grated onion, the remaining olive oil, salt, pepper and all but a tablespoon or so of the chives, which you should reserve for the garnish.

Mix all the ingredients thoroughly.

Grease the tart trays, if you are using, or your baking tray, and place the potato mixture in each section, pressing firmly down so that each rösti is well compacted. If using a baking tray, place a small handful of the potato mix between the palms of your hands and press together until it is well compacted. Place on the tray and cook for about 30 minutes or until golden brown.

Serve garnished with a dollop of sour cream, chives and some freshly ground black pepper on top.

# BAKED CAMEMBERT

## WITH ROSEMARY, THYME AND SOLDIERS

———

*A whole 250g circular Camembert in a wooden box ~ 6–8 small sprigs of rosemary ~ large pinch of fresh thyme ~ freshly ground black pepper ~ 1 ciabatta loaf, sliced into chunky strips about 10cm x 2cm each ~ 2 tbsp olive oil ~ handful of chopped fresh chives* **TO SERVE:** *apple slices ~ grapes ~ onion chutney*

A warm, rich, meltingly soft Camembert has the kind of oozy consistency that is best eaten with crunchy sticks of bread baked with olive oil – a grown-up version of sticking soldiers in your boiled egg. The herbs give the dish a wonderful aroma. If your bread is stale, so much the better.

Cooking doesn't get any simpler than this.

**Milton's Method** ☞ Preheat the oven to 180°C/gas mark 4. Remove any plastic packaging from the Camembert, line the wooden box with a little greaseproof paper and put the cheese back in.

Score several slits across the top of the cheese with a sharp knife and poke in the rosemary sprigs. Sprinkle the thyme and a couple of grinds of black pepper over the top. Place on a baking tray.

Prepare the bread by brushing each 'soldier' all over with olive oil and placing on a baking tray. Bake the cheese and the bread in the oven for 15–20 minutes, or until the centre of the cheese has melted and the bread is crisp and golden.

Sprinkle the chives over the cheese and serve immediately with thin wedges of tart eating apples, grapes and onion chutney.

# BRUSCHETTA

WITH OLIVES
AND ANCHOVIES

———

(makes approximately 25 bruschette) *1 French baguette, cut into 1cm thick slices ~ 4 tbsp good quality olive oil ~ 3 cloves garlic, finely chopped ~ 1 x 400g tin chopped tomatoes ~ approx. 35 green olives, thinly sliced ~ approx. 25 white anchovy fillets ~ salt and pepper*

All the best accompaniments to drinking are salty and this is no exception – crispy, baked baguettes topped with a garlicky tomato sauce, anchovies and olives. Super simple and super tasty.

**Milton's Method** ☞  Preheat the oven to 160°C/gas mark 3. Brush the slices of bread with olive oil and place on a baking tray. Bake for about 10 minutes, until lightly toasted. Be careful not to overcook.

Place a frying pan on a medium heat and pour in the rest of the olive oil. Add the garlic and cook for a minute or so, stirring, until it is just beginning to change colour. Add the tomatoes and stir well. Season to taste. Turn the heat down and simmer for 20 minutes, stirring occasionally. The liquid will reduce and the tomatoes will become a thick paste.

Spread the paste on the bruschetta and top with the sliced olives and a single piece of anchovy per slice.

# CROSTINI

## WITH TUNA AND
## CAPER BERRIES

(makes approximately 24 crostini) *1 baguette, sliced into 1cm pieces ~ 2 tbsp olive oil ~ 2 x 110g tins of pole caught tuna in olive oil ~ 6 tinned anchovy fillets ~ 2 tbsp capers ~ 1 tbsp grated lemon zest ~ 1 clove garlic ~ 110g mascarpone cheese ~ handful of kalamata olives, pitted and halved ~ handful of parsley, roughly chopped ~ 24 caper berries*

Yes, caper berries are those things that you only ever normally see at drinks receptions and parties when a real person isn't picking up the tab. And these are the kind of smart canapé (if slightly on the larger side) that you might see at such a do. I'm not entirely sure if there is a difference between crostini and bruschetta, but this one is crostini. Definitely. At least, I definitely think so.

**Milton's Method** ☞ Preheat the oven to 160°C/gas mark 3. Brush the slices of bread on both sides with olive oil and place on a baking tray. Bake for about 10 minutes, but be careful not to overcook them.

Combine all the other ingredients except for the caper berries in a blender, including the oil from the tuna. Blitz into a smooth paste.

When you're almost ready to serve the crostini (do it too early and they'll lose their crispness), spread the mixture on the bread and top each slice with a caper berry.

'One should always
be drunk. That's
all that matters...
But with what? With
wine, with poetry,
or with virtue, as you
chose. But get drunk.'

Charles Baudelaire

# ENGLISH CHEESE FONDUE

WITH PERRY

—

*500g of a mixture of coarsely grated cheese such as extra mature cheddar, Cheshire, Red Leicester and Double Gloucester ~ ½ tsp Coleman's mustard powder ~ 175ml medium dry perry (e.g. Hogan's Vintage Perry) ~ 2 tsp cornflour ~ 2 tbsp single cream ~ 1 tbsp cider brandy or pear brandy (or French brandy if you have neither of these) ~ freshly ground black pepper* **TO SERVE:** *ingredients for dipping e.g. brown toast, gherkins, pickled cauliflower, apple slices and celery stalks*

After a hard day of work (or play), a fondue is a great thing to share with friends. Hell, let's get cheesy as anything and call it a 'fun-do', because you can't help but have a cartoon grin on your face when you're eating it. It is possible to make a great fondue using English, rather than French or Swiss, cheeses and English perry, rather than white wine, which is what I have done here.

This is best if you have a spirit burner that you can place on a table with a fondue pan or saucepan on top as you need to keep the fondue warm to prevent it from solidifying.

**Milton's Method** ☞ Toss the cheese with the mustard powder and set aside to reach room temperature.

Pour the perry into a saucepan and heat to just before boiling point. Remove from the heat and tip in half of the cheese. Stir the cheese into the perry with a wooden spoon, using a backward and forward motion rather than a circular one to avoid splitting the mixture.

Return the saucepan to a low heat, stirring all the time. Add the remaining cheese gradually until it is all melted. Mix the cornflour with the single cream and add it to the mixture, then stir to thicken. Add the brandy and season with pepper. Tranfer the saucepan to the burner or pour the mixture into the fondue pot.

Serve with small bite-size chunks of wheatmeal toast or granary bread rolls, gherkins, pickled cauliflower, segments of apple, sticks of celery and anything else you fancy, using fondue forks if you have them, or skewers if you don't.

# STEAK HACHÉ SLIDERS

## ON TOASTED BRIOCHE

*(makes 12 sliders) 600g coarsely minced steak with good fat content (not too lean) ~ salt and pepper ~ olive oil, for brushing ~ 1 x 400g loaf sliced brioche ~ red onion chutney* **TO SERVE:** *12 small slices bleu d'Auvergne* **YOU WILL NEED:** *circular pastry cutter, approx. 6.5cm in diameter ~ cocktail sticks*

The quality of the end product here depends entirely on the quality of the meat. There are no tricks or gimmicks with steak haché – unlike a burger it is just pure beef.

A slider is a small burger, much loved of restaurants with high margins. The advantage when making them yourself is that they make ideal party food, rather than a meal in itself. Here, the quantities are for a dozen sliders: two dozen morsels of sweet brioche, sandwiched together with savoury meat, sharp blue cheese and slightly acidic chutney.

**Milton's Method** ☞ In a large bowl, season the meat well with salt and pepper and mix in with your hands. Using a circular pastry cutter placed on a plate, press the meat down inside it to a depth of about 2–2.5 centimetres. Make 12 patties this way.

Place some oil in a small bowl and brush each steak patty with oil on the upper side. Heat a cast-iron skillet and, when it's very hot, add your sliders, oiled side down, pressing down a little with the back of a metal slice. While they're cooking brush the other side with oil.

Brush the brioche with olive oil and toast under a grill until golden then, using the pastry cutter, cut the brioche to the same size as the burgers. Spread onion chutney on one side of 12 toasted brioche slices.

For rare, cook your patties for 2–3 minutes on each side so that they're just seared on the outside. A medium burger will be about 5 minutes per side.

Place the burgers on top of the chutney side of the brioche, add a slice of bleu d'Auvergne to each, put the hat of the slider on top and skewer with a cocktail stick to keep in place.

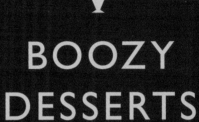

# BOOZY
# DESSERTS

—

Alcohol and pudd
marriage. Desserts
what can be more
a few units of alco
fantastically unheal
if you don't add a
dessert, then ther
of having one of a
drinks with it, or
appearance of dess
is the sign of a me
and is ending on th

make a perfect
r us indulgence and
ulgent than pouring
over your already
final course? Even
nol to your actual
always the option
normous range of
r it, or both: the
wines and digestifs
that has gone well
best possible note.

# CRÊPES
# TOM FOSTER

—

**FOR THE CRÊPES:** *55g flour ~ pinch of salt ~ 1 egg ~ 100ml milk ~ 35ml water ~ 30g butter* **FOR THE BANANAS:** *50g butter ~ 125g brown sugar ~ ½ tsp ground cinnamon ~ 4 tbsp banana liqueur (Bols or De Kuyper) ~ 4 bananas, peeled, topped and tailed and cut lengthways into 4 segments ~ 4 tbsp dark rum* **TO SERVE:** *vanilla ice cream*

Bananas, at least to my mind, need a bit of booze and sugar and spice to make them nice. Bananas Foster, named after a member of New Orleans crime commission from the 1950s, Richard Foster, is a great staple recipe from the New Orleans Kitchens restaurant. The French culture that left so great a mark on New Orleans suggested another possible variation on this dessert to me – turning the bananas into a filling for crêpes which I've decided to name after my great friend – and Francophile – Tom Foster.

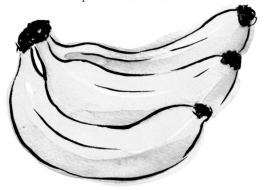

**Milton's Method ☞** Make the batter for the crêpes by sifting the flour and a pinch of salt into a large bowl and making a well in the centre. Break the egg into the well and whisk it with a fork, gradually incorporating the flour. Mix the milk and the water together and add them to the flour gradually, incorporating all the flour and whisking with the fork until the batter is smooth. Rest the batter in the fridge for about 15 minutes.

For the banana mixture, heat a frying pan over a medium flame, add the butter, sugar and cinnamon and cook until the sugar has dissolved and the sauce is a deep caramel colour. Add the banana liqueur and the banana pieces. Move the banana pieces around the pan until they start to colour. Add the rum and, carefully, tilt the pan to flambé (flame) the liqueur. Mind your eyebrows! Take the pan off the heat and set it aside.

In a separate frying pan, melt some butter over a medium-high heat. Pour a ladleful of batter into it, quickly swirling the pan so it spreads as thinly as possible across the bottom of the pan.

Cook the crêpe for about 45 seconds to 1 minute before flipping to cook the other side. Don't bother turning it with a palette knife. Flip it. It's worth taking a risk or two in life. Cook for another 30–45 seconds until golden and remove from the pan to a warmed plate. Add some more butter and repeat.

When the crêpes are ready, fill with the banana mixture and serve with ice cream.

# CARAMELISED RUM MANGO

WITH VODKA LIME JELLY
AND GINGERNUT CRUMBLE

———

*1 packet lime jelly ~ vodka, to taste ~ 4 tbsp sugar ~ 1 tbsp dark rum ~ 1 tbsp water ~ 1 vanilla pod, halved and seeds scraped out ~ 1 mango, peeled, cored and sliced ~ 2 tsp lime juice ~ 4 gingernut biscuits, lightly crushed*

Tropical fruits have always been one of my favourite things about visiting warmer climes and this boozy tropical fruit treat couldn't be simpler to make. Remember that the jelly needs to be made in advance to have time to set. And, remember too, that vodka jelly can get you extremely drunk, so use with caution!

**Milton's Method** ☞ Follow the packet instructions to make the lime jelly, but only use two-thirds the recommended amount of boiling water, then, once the jelly has dissolved, top up with the vodka. Depending on the strength you want, you can change the ratio of vodka to water. Pour the liquid jelly into ice cube moulds and place in the fridge to set.

Once the jelly has set, prepare the mango by heating the sugar, rum, water and vanilla seeds in a non-stick saucepan over a medium heat. It should come to the boil within a couple of minutes and begin to reduce and get sticky. Add the mango and make sure that all of it is coated in the caramel mixture as it continues to reduce. Take care not to burn the caramel. Once the mango is heated through and well coated with the mixture, remove the saucepan from the heat.

Place the mango on a plate, spooning any additional caramel over it. Squeeze a little lime juice over the top to freshen it up. Place a couple of cubes of lime jelly on the plate and sprinkle the gingernut crumble on the mango.

Eat while the mango is still warm.

# MILTON'S TIPSY TRIFLE

—

 (cinch)

*1 packet raspberry jelly ~ 250g frozen summer fruits ~ 1 piece star anise ~ 3 tbsp sugar ~ 16–20 lady's fingers ~ 4 tbsp blackcurrant jam ~ 125ml sweet sherry ~ 300ml thick ready-made custard ~ 200ml double cream ~ toasted flaked almonds*

There are few things more British than a trifle soaked in sherry with thick custard and cream and summer fruits (even though this recipe is made with French lady's fingers). I've used thick, ready-made fresh custard in the recipe as the tedium of making it myself was too much to bear. If you are less lazy than me, then by all means start cracking those eggs. This trifle should be served in a glass dish so that you can see the layers.

**Milton's Method** ☞ Make the jelly according to the packet instructions. Place in the freezer to set. Thaw the summer fruits in a small saucepan over a low heat with the star anise and the sugar. Stir a couple of times. When thawed, after 5 minutes, remove the star anise and allow the fruits to cool.

Layer half the lady's fingers on the bottom of a small glass pudding dish so that the surface is covered, then spread the jam over the top. Add another layer of sponge fingers then pour the sherry over the top. Add the summer fruits mix, then a layer of custard. Break up the jelly and spread it on top of the custard, then layer more custard on top. Whip the cream until thick then layer it over the custard and garnish with the flaked almonds.

Leave in the fridge to set for 1–2 hours before serving.

# PANETTONE

WITH PEDRO XIMENEZ, SULTANAS,
ALMONDS AND ICE CREAM

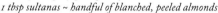

(cinch)

*2 large slices of panettone ~ 100ml Pedro Ximenez*
*~ 1 tbsp soft brown sugar ~ squeeze of lemon juice*
*~ 2 large scoops of good quality vanilla ice cream ~*
*1 tbsp sultanas ~ handful of blanched, peeled almonds*

I admit to not being an expert in panettone, so it may be that the
varieties I've been given as gifts have not been the best, but I've often
found them to be overly dry and airy. My handy solution to this
problem – as is often the case in a crisis – has been to soak the thing
in booze. I'm not too fussy about this and generally I have used
whatever I've got lying around at the time. This has included marsala,
dark rum, brandy and, memorably, sloe gin, but the best booze to
use to make a great pudding out of panettone, without a doubt, is Pedro
Ximenez or 'PX' – sweet, dark, raisin-y sherry.

**Milton's Method** ☞ Place the slices
of panettone in the serving bowls
and pour the Pedro Ximenez over
them. Leave to soak. Combine
the soft sugar with the lemon
juice in a separate bowl. Mix well.

Spoon the ice cream on top of the
panettone, then dribble the lemon
juice and sugar mixture on top of
the ice cream. Sprinkle the sultanas
and almonds over the top and serve
immediately.

# SHERRY AND GINGER LOG

## WITH PISTACHIO
## AND CHOCOLATE

—

*300ml double cream ~ 125ml medium dry sherry ~ 250g gingernut buscuits ~ 2 tbsp pistachio nuts, shelled and roughly chopped ~ 1 tbsp crystallised stem ginger, roughly chopped ~ 75g good quality dark chocolate, shaved*

This is a retro treat that my dear mother used to cook, back in the days when people still believed that double cream was a healthy snack. I actually do think that double cream is healthy so long as it's eaten in the right proportion with everything else. One of my mottos is to never, ever, choose low-fat varieties of anything when a full-fat one is available: the full-fat one is always much tastier.

This pudding should be prepared in advance and chilled in the fridge for a few hours to set.

**Milton's Method** ☞ In a large mixing bowl, whisk the cream until thickened and stiff. Fold 25ml of the sherry into the cream. Smear a line of cream down the centre of a serving plate. This will hold your confection in place.

Pour the remaining sherry into a small bowl. Dunk the biscuits into the sherry one by one. This has to be judged carefully – dip too briefly and your biscuit will not soak up enough sherry. Dip for too long and your biscuit will disintegrate. I recommend something along the lines of: dip – one-elephant, two-elephant – and remove. After you have dunked one biscuit, spread some of the cream on one side with a palette knife. Repeat this process, sticking the biscuits together with the cream and placing them on the plate until you have a 'log' shape.

Spread the remaining cream carefully and evenly over the entire log. Place in the fridge for 2–3 hours to set. Remove from the fridge and garnish with the pistachios, stem ginger and chocolate shavings.

*Et voilà!* Serve.

# THE BIG
# LEBOWSKI
# SUNDAE
—

*4 ice cubes ~ 60ml Kahlua ~ 60ml chilled vodka ~ 4 scoops vanilla ice cream ~ 1 carton condensed milk ~ 1 tbsp toasted crushed hazelnuts ~ 2 maraschino cherries*

Based on a classic white Russian cocktail, this is the kind of alcoholic ice-cream sundae that The Dude might approve of. It should have a strikingly layered effect with the coffee-coloured Kahlua at the bottom and the condensed milk and ice cream at the top. If you muddle the ingredients together it becomes something else entirely (a 'dirty bird'), which may or may not suit you, depending on your proclivities and your mood.

**Milton's Method** ☞  Take 2 chilled sundae glasses, or any other type of tall, slender glass that you might have to hand and put the ice cubes, Kahlua and vodka in them. Carefully place a scoop of ice cream in each so that it doesn't fall into the bottom of the glass but rests on top of the ice cubes, distinct from the dark Kahlua layer beneath.

Pour in condensed milk almost to the top of each glass. Add another scoop of ice cream, sprinkle with the toasted, crushed hazelnuts, add a teaspoon of Kahlua for colour, and top with a maraschino cherry to garnish.

# VITTLES
# AND VINE

—

Matching food and drink
each and is all the rage t
but also beer, cider an
marketeers look for ev
persuade us to part wit
number of these match
drinks industry manufact
for this book, dear reade
with Indian food' and 'wh
And, however cynical I
motives, and however ti
most egregious forms
occasionally revelatory: e
a few pairings that I hope
age you to experiment v

add a new dimension to
days, not just with wine
en whisky, as the booze
ore inventive ways to
r cash. I have been to a
events orchestrated by
s and retailers as research
ey included 'beer pairings
pairings with chocolate'.
have been about their
I got at listening to the
llshit, the results were
anies of taste. Here are
inspire you and encour-
your own combinations.

# A SIMPLIFIED ARNOLD BENNETT OMELETTE

WITH WHITE BURGUNDY

—

    (toil)

*200g smoked haddock, skin on ~ 250ml milk ~ 1 bay leaf ~ 12 peppercorns ~ 5 eggs ~ 100ml crème fraiche ~ small handful of tarragon, finely chopped ~ small handful of chives, finely chopped ~ knob of butter ~ 75g grated Parmesan ~ salt and pepper* **TO SERVE:** *2 handfuls of watercress*

*The Food*
This has a reputation of a rather difficult dish for the average domestic cook, but when stripped back to its basics – a creamy, cheesy, smoked-fish omelette – it certainly doesn't have to be and I have simplified my version of it as much as possible by eliminating the complex sauces. While something may be lost in doing this, remember: this dish was developed by chefs at the Savoy hotel. And let's face it, not all of us want to faff around pretending to be on MasterChef when there's fun to be had outside the kitchen. I have also added tarragon to give it a more distinctively French flavour that seems doubly appropriate when matched with white Burgundy.

**Milton's Method** ☞ Poach the haddock by simmering the milk in a saucepan with the bay leaf and the peppercorns for 8–10 minutes. Remove from the pan, drain well and flake the fish from the skin onto a plate, checking for bones, and set aside.

Separate one of your eggs and whisk the egg white in a bowl until you have soft peaks, then gradually fold in the crème fraiche and the tarragon. Set aside while you make the omelette. Whisk the remaining eggs in a bowl and season with salt, pepper and chives. Add the knob of butter to a heavy frying pan over a medium-high flame and, when melted and beginning to bubble, add the eggs to the pan. Use a slice to stop the omelette from sticking to the sides and cook until there is just a little residual runniness on the top.

Scatter the flaked haddock on top and pour the whisked egg white and crème fraiche mixture over the fish so it covers the entire omelette. Cover with the Parmesan and place under a hot grill until golden brown. Serve with watercress and a glass of Burgundy.

*The Drink*
Many of the most famous names of French wine including Mersault and Puligny Montrachet can be found in the Burgundy region between Dijon and Lyon. The white wines here are made from the chardonnay grape and go extremely well with creamy fish dishes. The only thing you'll have to watch is your wallet – Burgundy is a notoriously expensive wine.

# CURRIED MONKFISH AND MUSSELS

## WITH GEWÜRZTRAMINER

*2 pieces of monkfish tail, each about 150g, skinned and boned ~ 3 tsp curry powder ~ 2 leeks, washed, halved lengthways and chopped into semi-circular pieces ~ 2 tbsp olive oil ~ pinch of saffron ~ 500g mussels, cleaned and with beards removed ~ 100ml dry white wine ~ 1 bay leaf ~ 2 sprigs of thyme ~ 100ml double cream ~ salt and pepper* **TO SERVE:** *French bread or mashed potato ~ wilted spinach*

## The Food

A simple, elegant dish curried in the French style i.e., with the simple addition of curry powder, saffron and cream, rather than with a whole combination of deep flavours and spices. Monkfish is expensive but delicious, with a uniquely firm texture.

**Milton's Method** ☞ Heat the oven to 180°C/gas mark 4. Remove the thin grey membrane from the monkfish. Dust the fillets with 2 teaspoons of the curry powder and a good pinch of salt (about ½ a teaspoon). Set aside.

Sautée the leeks very gently in a little olive oil with the remaining curry powder and a pinch of saffron. Meanwhile, heat an ovenproof frying pan over a medium-high heat and add a tablespoon of olive oil then the monkfish fillets. Cook for about 3 minutes, or until they have coloured all over, then pop the pan into the oven for 5 minutes.

While the monkfish is in the oven, cook the mussels. Heat a deep saucepan over a medium heat and add the mussels, wine, bay leaf and thyme. Cover and shake. The mussels should take about 4 minutes to cook.

Remove the mussels from the heat (discarding any that haven't opened) and add the cooking liquor from the mussels to the pan with the leeks in it. Let the sauce reduce a little then add the cream and season with salt and pepper. Stir thoroughly and simmer on a low heat for a couple of minutes while you assemble the other ingredients.

The fish is ready when it's firm to the touch. Remove it from the oven and set aside. If you have time, and you want your plate to look smart, remove the mussels from their shells. Pour the creamy leek sauce into shallow bowls, add the fish and scatter the mussels around it. Serve either with some warm French bread to mop up the sauce or creamy mashed potato and wilted spinach.

*The Drink*
Gewürztraminer is a wonderfully fruity and aromatic white wine that is most popularly associated with the Alsace region of France, though good examples can also be found from Chile, New Zealand and North America. It is commonly paired with spicy dishes and works especially well with the cream, saffron and the curry powder in this recipe.

# SALT COD
# CROQUETTES

WITH MANZANILLA

———

*300g salt cod fillet ~ 450ml milk ~ ½ onion, sliced ~ a few peppercorns ~ 1 bay leaf ~ 150g mashed potato ~ handful of parsley, finely chopped ~ 2 tsp lemon juice ~ 50g plain flour ~ 2 eggs, beaten ~ 150g fine white breadcrumbs ~ vegetable oil, for frying ~ salt and pepper* **TO SERVE:** *garlic mayonnaise ~ rocket*

## The Food
Salt cod is dry and needs to be rehydrated and desalted. Soak it for 24 hours before use, in several changes of water. The croquettes are a common tapas dish in Spain and make great drinking food: crispy on the outside, moist and salty within.

**Milton's Method** ☞ Poach the cod in the milk with the sliced onion, peppercorns and bay leaf for 15 minutes, then gently flake the fish into a bowl, removing any bones.

Combine the mashed potato, cod, parsley and lemon juice in a large bowl and season generously to taste. Break the mixture into several small balls – you should get 8–10. Then elongate slightly so you have something like small, rounded cylinders. Roll in the flour, then in the beaten egg and finally in the breadcrumbs. Heat 1.5 centimetres of vegetable oil in a frying pan over a medium-high heat, and when hot, add the croquettes and fry until golden and crisp. Serve with garlic mayonnaise and rocket.

## The Drink
Manzanilla is a type of dry fino sherry that's perfect with fish. It is produced near the sea and there is an element of saltiness to it (it is often described as 'briny') that especially lends itself to drinking with seafood.

'I cook with wine, sometimes I even add it to the food.'

W. C. Fields

# SEARED SCALLOPS, SMOKED LARDONS AND BLACK PUDDING

WITH PORTER

—

*8 scallops (4 per person), including 'coral' ~ knob of butter ~ 8 rounds of black pudding, about 1cm thick ~ 100g smoked lardons ~ large handful of rocket ~ juice of 1 lemon ~ drizzle of extra virgin olive oil ~ salt and pepper*

## The Food

Scallops have become one of the most essential of all ingredients in fashionable modern gastronomy. There is good reason for it – at their best they're sweet, juicy and delicious. Smoked lardons, black pudding and a few rocket leaves here provide the perfect foil.

**Milton's Method** ☞ Pat the scallops dry with some kitchen paper and season well with salt and pepper. Melt a generous knob of butter in a heavy frying pan on a high heat and sear the black pudding on both sides. Put on a warm plate and set aside.

Cook the lardons in the same pan until crisp and golden. Drain on kitchen paper. Now sear the scallops – about 90 seconds on one side, 30 seconds on the other. They should be golden on the surface. The coral should be opaque and firm to the touch.

Arrange the scallops on a plate with the black pudding. Sprinkle the lardons and the rocket over them. Deglaze the pan with the lemon juice, add a little olive oil and drizzle the pan juices over the top of the scallops. Serve straight away.

*The Drink*
Porter is a dark, rich, complex beer that's usually fairly strong
– between 5 and 6.5%. It is an excellent match for scallops
and oysters. Two good examples are Fuller's London Porter
and Meantime London Porter.

# STUFFED GRILLED MUSSELS

WITH INNIS AND
GUNN BLONDE

———

*24 mussels, cleaned and debearded ~ 50ml dry sherry ~ 50g butter ~ 1 shallot, finely diced ~ 50g plain flour ~ 250ml milk ~ 125ml white wine ~ handful of parsley, finely chopped ~ 50g fresh breadcrumbs ~ 50g finely grated Parmesan ~ salt and pepper*

*The Food*
Buy the biggest mussels you can find for this recipe – succulent mussels in their shell with a creamy sauce and a crisp Parmesan crust on top.

**Milton's Method** ☞ Cook the mussels in a saucepan with 50ml of sherry and the lid on. This takes just 3 minutes. Remove the pan from the heat and discard any mussels that haven't opened.

In another pan melt the butter and cook the shallot over a medium heat. When the shallot has softened, add the flour and stir in. Cook for a minute then add the milk gradually, stirring constantly to remove any lumps. When all the milk is incorporated, and the sauce has thickened a little, add the wine. Cook for another 5–7 minutes, until the alcohol has evaporated and the sauce is thickened and almost gooey. Season to taste. Add the parsley.

Remove and discard the upper shell of each mussel. Place the mussels on a baking tray and spoon a little sauce onto each.

Combine the breadcrumbs and the Parmesan and sprinkle over the mussels. Place under a hot grill until the breadcrumbs have turned crisp and golden.

## The Drink

Innis and Gunn Blonde is a pale, golden beer that is aged in oak barrels. The flavour is quite unlike any other beer that I have tasted. The first time I tried it was with oysters and it was a perfect fit. Toffee and vanilla are underscored by malt, oak and citrus, that together provide a perfect match for shellfish.

# VENISON SAUSAGES

WITH CIDER SAUCE
AND SCRUMPY

———

*2 tbsp olive oil ~ 2 onions, roughly chopped ~ 2 large eating apples, peeled and*
*roughly chopped ~ ½ butternut squash, peeled and roughly chopped ~ 6 good*
*quality venison sausages ~ 1 tbsp thyme, roughly chopped ~ 2 sprigs of rosemary*
*~ 1 tbsp plain flour ~ 300ml cider ~ 250ml chicken stock ~ salt and pepper*
**TO SERVE:** *mashed potato ~ kale, spinach or sprouts*

## The Food
I've spent a fair bit of time living in the New Forest in southern
England and this simple recipe represents some of the flavours from
the area that mean the most to me, mainly venison, cider and apples.

**Milton's Method** ☞ Heat your oven to 220°C/gas mark 7. Warm
some olive oil in a baking tray and keep the tray over a medium flame
as you add the onions, apple, squash, sausages, thyme and rosemary.
Season generously with salt and pepper. Shake everything about
reasonably vigorously. When everything is well coated with oil and
seasoning, place the baking tray in the mid/upper part of the oven
and cook for 30–40 minutes, turning the sausages once or twice.

When everything is cooked, the squash and onions should just be
beginning to caramelise and the sausages should be well browned.
Set the sausages aside in a warm place and put three quarters of the
vegetables in a warm serving dish. Remove the sprigs of rosemary.

To make a gravy, place the baking tray on the hob with a low heat,
add the flour to the fat at the bottom of the pan and stir it in until it
is well blended in and you have a pale-looking paste. Mash some of
the squash and apple into the mix as you go. Add a little of the cider
and stir vigorously into the paste, until it thickens. Keep adding more
scrumpy, making sure that the cider is well absorbed and the liquid

thickens. Once all the cider has been
added, bring quickly to the boil and simmer
for a minute or two, stirring all the while, before adding the stock.
Bring back up to the boil again and let it simmer for 10 minutes,
stirring occasionally, reducing and thickening. If the gravy gets too
thick add a little water. Strain through a colander, mashing the
vegetables through. Serve the sausages with the vegetables, gravy,
mashed potato and greens like kale, spinach or sprouts.

*The Drink*

Proper scrumpy always has a home-made feel to it. You should almost
be able to taste the hay in the barn in which it was made. Unlike
many mass-market commercial ciders, it should taste of apples. It
might be cloudy and vary in hue from pale yellow to bright orange.
It should be strong – at least 6% ABV. My favourite colour of scrumpy
is the kind of gold that the trees sometimes turn in autumn – a deep,
rich colour that's somewhere between a setting sun and sunlight
through a brackish stream. I have made my own scrumpy very
successfully and if you have a ready supply of apples I suggest you try
it too (please refer to disclaimers at various points in this book).

I have drunk plenty of a New Forest cider referred to as 'Tight
Hat Cider' by the maker's son. He says that: 'After a couple of
pints of it, I feel like I'm wearing a very tight hat.' This is proper
scrumpy: stuff that has strange, unquantifiable properties and that
may make you do unexpected things. Like the wobbly leg cider I
had in Wiltshire. Or that stuff in Sussex I tried where I got naked
and found myself hiding... Oh, but wait, that's another story. For
another time.

## Acknowledgements

Thanks to all my drinking companions, past and present, who have helped, however unwittingly, in the creation of this book. It is a long list so I shan't mention all of them. They know who they are.

Particular thanks to my agent, Andrew Gordon and his assistant Marigold Atkey at David Higham Associates, and to Rosemary Davidson and Simon Rhodes at Random House, for all their hard work in helping this book to publication.

Thanks also to all those who tried, tested and suggested recipes including Simon and Rosalind Gould, Henry Riley and Lisa Brackenridge, Anna and Tommy Macken, Jimmy and Tomo Robertson, Helen and Chris Davis and Sue and Steve Telfer, Michael and Billi Ksela and Wolfgang Ritter.

It has been a pleasure working with the very talented illustrators and designers Katie Morgan, Matt Baxter and Graeme Rodrigo who have made this book as beautiful as it is.

Last, but quite the opposite to the least, thanks to Bridget and Gilbert for all their love and support.

## Final disclaimer

Please get drunk responsibly. And know your limits. Especially in the kitchen.

We (the author and publisher) will not accept any responsibility for your drunken condition, your experimentation in the kitchen (based on the contents of this book or otherwise), nor for any implications for your health arising thereof.

The author has thoroughly researched all the recipes in this book and, to the best of his knowledge, believes the ingredients, quantities and methods to be entirely correct. He will not accept responsibility for any attempts at his recipes that fail.

We wish you the best of luck. You may well need it.

## All about Milton

Milton Crawford made a name for himself with *The Hungover Cookbook* (2010), which brought him global notoriety, and soon after (in 2011) he won the Bombardier Beer Writer of the Year. His passion for alcohol is matched by his love of food, travel, pubs and the outdoors. He finds that a strict regimen of exercise helps him to drink and eat greater amounts, recover faster and come back for more, sooner; this regime was, at least in part, inspired by the 2012 London Olympics. Thanks, Sebastian.

He believes, along with Baudelaire, that intoxication is an essential precondition of creative life. Alcohol is not entirely necessary for this, but for those lacking in imagination and means, it is the most readily available vehicle.

Milton divides his time between London, the New Forest, Austria and India, hoping that if he is able to spread himself thinly enough across enough of the planet, he will merge into some higher form of consciousness. This has not happened yet.

Milton stopped tweeting @miltoncrawford (as he tweeted using the same hand as he was using to hold his glass, and it all got too much) but may start again at some point in the future.